Choosing to Love

Jerry & Barbara Cook

A Division of GL Publications
Ventura, CA U.S.A.

Other good reading:

Love, Acceptance and Forgiveness by Jerry Cook with Stanley C. Baldwin

Communication: Key to Your Marriage by H. Norman Wright

Pillars of Marriage by H. Norman Wright

The foreign language publishing of all Regal books is under the direction of Gospel Literature International (GLINT). GLINT provides financial and technical help for the adaptation, translation and publishing of books for millions of people worldwide. For information regarding translation contact: GLINT, P.O. Box 6688, Ventura, California 93006.

Scripture quotations in this publication are from the *New International Version,* Holy Bible. Copyright © 1978 by the New York International Bible Society. Used by permission. Also quoted is the Authorized King James version.

Published by Regal Books
A Division of GL Publications
Ventura, California 93006
Printed in U.S.A.

Library of Congress Cataloging in Publication Data

Cook, Jerry.
Choosing to love.

1. Marriage—Religious aspects—Christianity.
I. Cook, Barbara II. Title.
BV835.C65 248.8'4 81-84566
ISBN-0-8307-0818-9 AACR2

Contents

BEGINNINGS/Barbara

Jerry and I are writing because we think we have something to say to you. This book is to share where we are right now in our growth together in the adventure of marriage. We do not come as experts or professionals who have all the answers. We come risking ourselves quite thoroughly, and with a little timidity about putting in print some of the personal letters and free verse that are so much a part of our way of communicating. We want to do this because we think there are many Christian couples struggling with the kinds of things we've felt; couples who, perhaps like us, couldn't exactly verbalize what's wrong. By a certain "Christian" standard you have the ideal marriage. But it's a marriage you hate, no matter what you've heard in sermons!

Some of our friends have suggested that we are not very "normal." You can decide that for yourself as you read these pages. We *feel* quite normal, have four normal children, a noisy dog, and live in a normal house on a busy suburban street. We tend to think that preachers and wives of preachers are fairly typical people, but we do accept the fact that all the world does not believe that. There is a mystical fantasy that pastors never have marriage problems, have perfect wives and perfect offspring at all times. We've never felt obliged to live by that fantasy, but we have discovered that because of it, it's kind of hard to find an understanding ear if you do have a problem, even if it's quite a small one. Maybe that's why my nagging little questions bothered me, drove me to the Word for answers, and to besieging heaven with lonely, agonized prayers very similar to the ones you read in Psalms. Many of these turned into music, sometimes wordless piano sonatas, and sometimes songs like this one that wrote itself one early morning:

Holy Spirit be my teacher,
Holy Spirit be my guide.
I am poor and often wondering—
I so need you by my side.

Holy Spirit be my comfort,
I so need your loving hand.
You're my only source of wisdom,
Only hope in which to stand.

Like a child, I search for answers
To the questions of our time.
I can only know in measure,
Must have more than my own mind.

Holy Spirit be my teacher,
Holy Spirit be my guide.
You are all eternal wisdom.
Be my comfort, be my guide.

It took a long time for me to realize Jerry didn't like

our marriage either. And still longer to learn how we could talk about that without guilt, without blaming each other, and without despising all the good things God had given us. We really had nothing to be unhappy about—no great stresses or tragedies to test our love, no crushing indebtedness, or emotional overload. There would certainly be no valid reason for divorce. Except that at times we felt so far away from each other that we wondered if a divorce of sorts had already taken place. Maybe you can understand that. If you can't, then maybe it will never happen to you—and I hope it doesn't. But perhaps the things we found out will be valuable if that feeling descends upon your relationship at times. At least we want to say to you, It doesn't have to be fatal!

What caused this "creeping separateness"? It would be easy to speculate. We all do quite well analyzing the cause and effect relationships of other people's problems. Well, it wasn't "the pressures of the ministry." Nor the expectations of church people that we be perfect or live up to a saintly image. East Hill Church is very large in numbers, that's true. But it is also very large on loving. And in Jerry's book, *Love, Acceptance and Forgiveness,* he just begins the story of that very wonderful body of people. The story continues to the present day and this book, if you keep reading, will show how those same people have grown in capacity to love, accept and forgive even their pastors, who had the audacity to tear apart and put back together their own marriage very publicly. The tapes of all those messages are available as live evidence that the Holy Spirit continues His work in our midst, including the work of transforming our most private relationships into love, acceptance and forgiveness.

Others may read this and speculate that growth or education, success or pride caused the problem. Or travel, or busyness. Or my ministry, my intellectual curiosity, or our friends, or our individuality. Perhaps we married too young or were too unprepared. None of those things are true. We love the ministry, and especially *our* church and *our* people. I thoroughly delight in being a pastor's wife and steadfastly resist all attempts at making that a role or stereotype. For me it has been a doorway to opportunity, a happy and full life, with few constrictions.

And no, we do not have a history of sexual hangups, interfering parents or bickering or jealousy. Here's what *we* think was wrong, what we believe separated us from each other emotionally and mentally: OUR CONCEPT OF MARRIAGE. We had, as probably many Christian couples do, a very inconsistent theology of marriage. Living, without realizing it, by a standard we did not really believe, which had been handed us by the current culture. Until we could begin facing all our assumptions about male and female roles, about the total woman and total man, fulfillment, love, commitment and other such concepts, we were each seeing the other through a grid of conditioning which obscured the real person. Some of our struggles were painful and you'll see glimpses of that on the pages where we speak personally. But it became very important to me to ask, "God, what is marriage supposed to be? How do you see us? Show me my blind spots; show me the difference between my romantic ideals and true reality!"

This is hard for public speakers; after all, we run the risk that we may have taught something in the past that was not quite accurate. And both of us have taught much on the subject of marriage, not only in our church but at conferences and retreats. In my broadcasts, one week each month is devoted to Bible studies regarding marriage. For many years I have taught in the college-age group of East Hill, and often about marriage, singleness and male-female relationships. It was not easy to face the fact that some of the truths I had confidently declared may have been tinged with unscriptural assumptions and clichés. The students themselves had plenty of questions about the traditional views of marriage presented by our evangelical churches. But those I could have stubbornly ignored, if it weren't for the restless dissatisfaction with my own "good marriage" and the growing hope that God might have something better than what we now knew. This little bit of hope persisted and led me to rethink and restudy the Scriptures with an openness I had never experienced before.

I began to notice how easily we Christians accept platitudes that are really godless observations on the way things are. We even manage to find Scripture verses to justify concepts contradictory to Christianity, such as "might makes right," "the end justifies the means," or "the way things are is the way things are meant to be." For me it became intensely vital to ask, "Which of my presuppositions are simply philosophies and values of our culture? And which of these beliefs represent true reality? Which align with God's values?"

Secular thinking, having no recognition of God at its base, has come up with alternative ways of explaining reality. It has logical systems of thought to enable a person to try to survive without God. These "survival systems" are needed by people who have no personal God or belief in life after death. Alone in the universe, their survival ultimately will be linked with the survival of the fittest. They must design a way to survive and carefully live by that understanding for their own protection. For persons outside the family of God all relationships must, of necessity, take this into consideration.

There is legitimate concern for the balance of power, the stronger to rule and the weaker to serve. There is a real and hopelessly endless struggle between men and women, rich and poor, strong and weak, besides those struggles based on race, status, position, possession and selfishness.

But inside the family of God these old survival systems can be discarded. We can discover God's view of reality; our relationships can then rest on an entirely new base—the base of authentic love; a thought system that truly believes the other person's value to be as great as our own. Few Christians have yet to work out the implications of this in their friendships, families and marriages. This book describes our concepts of how it can be worked out and our own efforts at living what we believe.

We will talk about authentic, strong Christian men relating to authentic, strong Christian women. We will not describe methods of playing male and female roles, nor list 10 keys to keeping mates happy. This book will not tell wives how to be subtle, fascinating or manipulative. It will not inspire husbands to pretend Superman talents. If it inspires Christian men and women, we hope it will be to learn to relate as real people. Real people are not afraid of emotions, desires, doubts or weaknesses when they draw on the strength and power of the indwelling Saviour. In Christ men and women can allow themselves to grow together.

Of course these pages contain only a small part of what we have learned so far. We realize we may raise questions for which we do not here provide answers—even answers we may have found satisfactory and would want to share. For that dilemma we find ourselves having to trust the Holy Spirit as your teacher, knowing He is dependable to pick those things of special value to you and teach them through our sharing. With that confidence in Him we offer ourselves in the chapters ahead.

Chapter 1/Barbara

What Is an "Ideal" Marriage?

If you were to ask a group of 20 people to share their definitions of friendship you would probably hear 20 different answers. I've noticed that the definitions vary with one's own needs: A person who is feeling lonely will say, "A friend is someone you can talk to"; a person who feels exploited will define it, "A friend is someone who loves you with no demands." Some people have narrow boundaries on friendship; others make them broad to include a large circle of people.

So it is with marriage. Those same 20 people would have 20 different definitions of what marriage is. All of us construct our own images of what an "ideal" marriage is based completely on what we have learned through other people—what we read, what we're taught, what we've seen and what our personal needs are.

Some people have a paternal image of marriage where the husband is an all-wise, ever-strong, benevolent king who teaches his wife, trains her how to please him, takes care of her and becomes her "all-in-all"—her sustenance, leader, master, lord.

Others construct a romantic image—all flowers and sweetness. The lovers gaze endlessly into each other's eyes, never quarrel and always feel warm and passionate emotions. If another person with this image evaluates your marriage and doesn't see such emotions emanating from you, then you fail his test—you definitely need help; you do not have a good marriage!

The various standards range from ownership to independence. Some standards call for a docile wife or an authoritarian husband; some call for an exacting partnership with the work evenly divided down the middle. Some standards are based only on the sexual creativity of the spouses; others are a reworking of some secular definition of friendship.

Which, if any, of those 20 definitions of an ideal marriage is the right one? Where do we find the perfect objective definition of this all-important relationship? All 20 definitions can't be right because each definer worked from the basis of his own individual needs; each became his own absolute. So, while I am evaluating my friends, or my spouse and marriage, by my own neat little list of standards, more than likely my friend or marital partner is not even aware of my standards. Furthermore, my friend or partner probably has his or her own list by which he or she is evaluating me! We can easily get caught up in our own definition so that we become judgmental of any marriage that falls short of our own standard.

Sue, a single lady of 24, moved into the home of a fine Christian family she met at church. Since Ted and Julie were leaders in her church, Sue assumed she would now observe, firsthand, the joys of a good Christian marriage. But soon she found reason to report that all was not well. Sue confided to the pastor that Ted and Julie didn't always "get along," that they were immature and Julie was not obedient to Ted.

Meanwhile, Ted and Julie were pleased with the growth they were experiencing together, happy that they were sharing their true feelings and learning to communicate. Who was right? By Sue's standards the marriage was falling apart! By Ted and Julie's standards the marriage was healthy and loving.

Earlier in my life I tended to respond defensively to other people's evaluations of our marriage and try to prove that I did in truth meet their "standard." Gradually I became aware of the hodgepodge of presuppositions and assumptions lying behind their standards and realized that it was dishonest, if not hopeless, for us to evaluate our marriage by their lists. Even then I found myself, at times, feeling a vague sense of guilt—not because I failed to meet *their* standards, but because I became aware that I was not even meeting the standards *I had set* for our marriage. For example, I liked romance and the ideal of a romantic marriage, but I considered all the days I had not behaved like Queen Guinevere!

I believed in the beauty of sexual creativity, but I was faced with the reality of those nights when I responded with little imagination.

I felt guilty about my communication failures (this guilt always comes at a time when one of us is confidently teaching on the subject of communication!).

I was discouraged with my insensitivity; marriage is supposed to have warmth and understanding, but sometimes I'm so obtuse!

In some ways my own standards were even more difficult to keep than were those of people who would evaluate my marriage. So I began asking things like, What is my standard for a good marriage? Do I really need a standard? Do I actually feel guilty about a set of rules that does not exist? Or guilty because I'm not *sure* what I believe? If I take it upon myself to assess someone else's marriage do I use my standard or theirs? Isn't there some divine standard somewhere that would wipe out all other standards? One that we could turn to whenever there is a question about an "ideal" marriage?

The Divine Standard

Now the Bible, of course, tells us what friendship is: A friend is someone who loves you or shows care or concern for you. Contrary to most of our thought patterns, the biblical usage is so broad that even a stranger can be a friend! Jesus' parable of the Good Samaritan indicates that showing hospitality to a stranger is an act of friendship. In fact, the definition of hospitality is just that—loving a stranger; sharing your goods with someone you haven't known before. The Greek word for friendship and love, *phileo,* is combined with the word for stranger, *xeno,* forming *philoxeno,* which is translated "hospitality." So, rather than defining friendship by what we want or need from others, the Bible defines friendship in terms of what we can do or give to others: *unconditional friendship.*

Now this definition of friendship is pretty easy to understand—although it is often hard to accept and follow through on. Now where in the Bible can I find a simple, cut-and-dried, 1-2-3 steps to an "ideal" marriage, one that doesn't require too much evaluation or decision-making on my part?

As you probably know, the Bible doesn't always provide an instant answer to all of life's questions. It would be great if the Bible was set up like a divine dictionary. How convenient if we could look at page 189 where the *M*s begin, read down to "Marriage" and find a concise sentence that ended "thus saith the Lord." Very rarely can we find in the Bible definite, concise guidelines for any of life's questions. Language is not that simple. And some words represent meanings too large to reduce into one terse sentence. Rather, God has chosen to teach us through ideas and concepts. He uses language that is understood in any time or culture. In some books God speaks through the mouths of fiery prophets; in others through analogies and similes.

Another dimension of the subject will be added as we read about it in poetic form, such as in Canticles or Psalms. Then we see Jesus living out the concept, or explaining it in parables. We see the early Christians dialoguing it in their Jerusalem councils. And finally in the triumphant Revelation the same concept will be presented repeatedly, like a glorious review, in symbolism taken from all the pages of the Old Testament.

Often it takes the whole Bible—the imagery and examples of both the Old and New Testaments—to show us what God thinks about a subject such as righteousness or love or justice—or marriage. And then it's as though God says softly, "*Now* do you get it? Have I said it in enough different ways that you can grasp my deeper meaning?"

The Divine Concept

The more I studied the Scriptures on the subject of marriage the more I realized that God has not imposed a rigid set of standards by which we must conform. I also realized that I didn't want a marriage based on a foundation of standards, rules for proper conduct, roles of husband and wife, obligations and duties which we should perform for each other. I didn't want my marriage to be like a basketball or football game. I wanted my marriage to be consistent with the divine concept of *unconditional love—agape.*

Now I had a new avenue of Scripture to follow. What is unconditional love? If the commitment to love another unconditionally is basic to a Christian concept of marriage, what are the rules that include all the demands love may make on me? Back to the Bible I went.

Ephesians 5 and 1 Peter 3 both give instructions on *expressing* unconditional love. And the entire book of Solomon's Song of Songs is a touching romance in poetic form. But even these descriptions are not all-inclusive *instructions* for how to have a good marriage, nor are they intended to be.

Then one day as I was again reading 1 Corinthians 13 I paraphrased the verses, inserting my name and my husband's name to make them more personal. When I was finished I realized I now could begin to see the divine concept of unconditional love. This became my commitment to God about how I want to relate to Jerry.

"For Barbara, loving Jerry means that she maintains a pattern of behavior toward him that always seeks his highest good and never his harm. Regardless of the ups and downs of her emotions, or the cost in time, energy or personal comfort, she will treat him with patience and kindness. She will not envy him, will not boast, will not relate on the basis of pride or ego struggles. She will not be rude to him—insulting or inconveniencing him. She will not be self-seeking but will be self-giving. She will not be easily angered with him or touchy or irritable. She will not hold grudges or resentments. She will not store bitterness toward him. She will not be pleased with any evil that happens to him but will rejoice with the truth. She always protects him, trusts him, hopes (believes in him), always perseveres. She is loyal to him—will defend him and endure in her commitment to him no matter what challenges arise to threaten that commitment. 'Now these three remain: faith, hope and love. But the greatest of these is love.' "

Our Father God is a far more merciful judge than are

His children; He doesn't have a list, or standards, to which we must conform to have an "ideal" marriage. His standard is *love, unconditional love.* That's the way He loves us—unconditionally. He does not base His love for us on which rules or regulations we keep. In fact, He says that there are no rules that can earn His love. Keeping the rules and regulations was the goal of the Pharisees; we live by a higher motive in life. Because Jesus loves us, accepts and forgives us, we can make a choice to love another human being in that same way. God tells us, through Jesus, that we are to love one another as He loves us (see John 15:12).

As Paul the apostle tells us in Galatians 3:24,25, "The law was put in charge to lead us to Christ that we might be justified by faith. Now that faith has come, we are no longer under the supervision of the law." Standards are sometimes useful to show up our imperfections, to let us see what sinners we really are. Like the Mosaic law, they cause us to face our true guilt and say, "I've failed; be merciful to me, a sinner!" But standards, like the Mosaic law, are not made to be kept—only to show us we can't keep them. We need a Saviour! We need God's grace; and we need grace from our partners.

I decided that for me an ideal marriage is one where I *choose* to love. Each new day I can renew my choice to love with a deep awareness of my tendency to fail, but simultaneously, an awareness of God's—and my husband's—grace.

Ideal Marriage: A Choosing to Love

I married a man I respect;
    I have no need to bow and defer.
I married a man I adore and admire;
    I don't need to be handed a list entitled
        "how to build his ego" or

"the male need for admiration."
Love, worship, loyalty, trust—these are inside me;
They motivate my actions.
To reduce them to rules destroys my motivation.
I *choose* to serve him
to enjoy him.
We *choose* to live together
and grow together,
to stretch our capacities for love
even when it hurts
and looks like conflict.
We *choose* to learn to know each other
as real people,
as two unique individuals
unlike any other two.
Our marriage is a commitment to love;
to belong to each other
to know and understand
to care
share ourselves
our goals
interests
desires
needs
Out of that commitment the actions follow.
Love defines our behavior
and our ways of living together.
And since we fail to meet not only the demands
of standards but also the
simple requirements of love
We are forced to believe in forgiveness
. . . and grace.

Bible Verses to Study for This Chapter

Descriptions of unconditional love: 1 Corinthians 13;

Ephesians 5:21-33; Song of Songs; 1 Peter 1:22; the book of Hosea.

Questions for Discussion

What do you think would be the difference between a marriage based on law and a marriage based on grace?

How does this coincide with a person's view of how he relates to God? (A person who relates to God through a set of laws often finds himself doubting God's love for him when he falls short of the standard. Is there a parallel in marriage?)

Does a commitment to love someone unconditionally mean I condone faults and sins in that person? Does unconditional love overlook sin or destructive character traits?

Many people make emotion-based commitments they cannot keep after the emotions cool. How can we be sure this is not what we're doing when we say, "I love you!"?

Chapter 2/Jerry

What Does God Have to Do with Marriage?

How did marriage fit into the creation process? Did God create men and women with marriage in mind? Is marriage a unique relationship or only one of many relationships among mankind?

In Mark 10:2-9 Jesus is asked about divorce. In His reply He appeals to God's original intention in creation. He declares that divorce was not in God's plan. " 'It was because your hearts were hard that Moses wrote you this law,' Jesus replied. 'But at the beginning of creation God "made them male and female." "For this reason a man will leave his father and mother and be united to his wife, and the two will become one flesh." So they are no longer two, but one. Therefore what God has joined together, let man not separate.' "

What is the "reason" to which Christ appeals? That God made them male and female? No. The simple fact of maleness and femaleness is not a strong enough base for the principles that follow Jesus' statement. In Greek upper-class marriages at this time there was no intention of the husband to cleave to his wife. She was the bearer of his legal children and the keeper of his house. But she was not considered his companion nor always his primary means of sexual fulfillment. There were other women suited and educated for these purposes. Just because males exist and females exist we can't automatically conclude, "Therefore, males and females should live together in a lifetime, monogamous marriage." In fact, this has *not* been the conclusion drawn in many societies. And in His culture it was an incredible statement for Jesus to make when He declared God's intentions for marriage to be: (1) permanent—never broken; (2) valued above even family and parental relationships; (3) unique in its unity of persons; (4) unique in its sexual union (one flesh). These radical views could not be based simply on the existence of maleness and femaleness. The "reason" Christ appeals to is God's intention in creation. An intention completely lost in the selfish fallen nature and compensated for by a poor substitute—divorce. Jesus said divorce was instituted by Moses because of fallen man's hardened heart—it was not so in the beginning.

God had something in mind when He created "man" as male and female. Woman was not an afterthought nor the final step to the male's completion. Both sexes were planned and created by God with profound intent.

Creation of Mankind

Genesis 1:26-31 records the acts of creation on the sixth day. That is the final day of creation and God's great world is crowned with the creation of mankind: "Then God said, 'Let us make man in our image, in our likeness, and let them rule over the fish of the sea and the birds of the air, over the livestock, over all the earth, and over all the creatures that move along the ground.' So God created man in his own image, in the image of God he created him; male and female he created them. God blessed them and said to them, 'Be fruitful and increase in number; fill the earth and subdue it. Rule over the fish of the sea and the birds of the air and over every living creature that moves on the ground.' Then God said, 'I give you every seed-bearing plant on the face of the whole earth and every tree that has fruit with seed in it. They will be yours for food. And to all the beasts of the earth and all the birds of the air and all the creatures that move on the ground—everything that has the breath of life in it—I give every green plant for food.' And it was so. God saw all that he had made, and it was very good. And there was evening, and there was morning—the sixth day."

In this first account of creation there is very little detail; Genesis 2 is more descriptive of creation events. But there are several things to notice in this first account.

The terms referring to man are plural. In verse 26 the plurality, "let *them* rule," is not a plurality of male creatures. God is referring to the fact that two kinds of persons will be created, and they are defined in verse 27 as male and female. This same idea is expressed again in Genesis 5:1,2: "When God created man, he made him in the likeness of God. He created them male and female."

Both the man and the woman are uniquely created. They do not share the common nature of all animals. They are made in the image and likeness of God. This creative act is in some sense a birth. God has vested Himself in these human creatures. This sets them forever apart from the rest of creation and at the same time relates them forever to Him.

In this, as in no other act of God, is the value of persons established. If we believe this we can be released from the struggle to find value by accomplishment. We are not valuable because of what we can do or achieve. We are valuable because we have been created in the image and the likeness of God. And this value is permanent—everlasting.

Both the man and the woman are created in God's image. The man by himself and the woman by herself are each created in His image and likeness. It does not take both of them to make a person. Their person resides in the fact of the creation. God has vested Himself in each of them. Their separate value is sealed—they are individually related to God.

Another thing to note—their authority is equal. They both are given the right to rule. They are given exactly the same things over which to rule. There is not one domain for the man and another for the woman. They both are told by God, "Be fruitful and increase in number; fill the earth and subdue it. Rule over the fish of the sea and the birds of the air and over every living creature that moves on the ground." God then proceeded to give them everything they needed for food and sustenance. In essence He gave them the entire earthly creation. God had spent five days creating it and now He made the whole thing a gift to this man and woman. Here is the coronation of the true rulers of this world!

It seems to me that the intentions of God in creating us are relatively uncomplicated. I would like to describe a principle that emerges from the opening chapters of the Bible. Simply stated it's this: Both men and women have equal value and are mutually dependent upon God and each other.

This does not mean that every person has to be married in order to fulfill God's plan. If so, Jesus in His chosen singleness would not be an example to us of the perfect man, a whole person who showed what we can be. As we will develop in a later chapter, singleness is a valid choice, although clearly it is not the choice most people will make. The desire to marry is such a strong part of our nature that those who set aside that desire in favor of other values are never a majority. The apostle Paul, who spoke much about the validity of singleness, including his own choice of that state, said that "woman is not independent of man, nor is man independent of woman" (1 Cor. 11:11). *The Living Bible* paraphrases it "in God's plan men and women need each other." So much for male chauvinism and for *female* chauvinism! The lifestyles of both Paul and Jesus were neither promiscuous nor ascetic as in an all-male community. Their lives illustrate respect for this understanding of male female interdependence.

Equal in Creation

Since the woman is given equal dominion with the man, with not the slightest qualification by God, we have to assume that she, as well as he, is equal to the task. It is almost a forgotten fact that the same leadership and authority qualities given to Adam to run this world were also given to Eve. Woman is no second-line ruler. There is full partnership given to equal and capable people—one a male, the other a female. It is also significant that while they are given the right to rule over all God's creation, they are *not* given the right to rule over one another. Because of the unique nature they each possess and their unique relationship with God and separateness from the rest of creation, their authority over creation does *not* include authority over one another.

(It is important too to realize that God's command to be fruitful and multiply came here in chapter 1, before the fall. This is why we do not believe the sexual act in marriage is somehow a shameful or less-intended part of God's purpose. The propriety of all creation, including the sexual relationship, is declared, "God saw all that he had made, and it was *very* good.")

In Genesis 2 we are given an in-depth look at how all this came about. As we study it, however, we must remember that the principles established from chapter 1 are not to be violated in our interpretation of chapters 2 and 3. Here are those principles as I see them in Genesis 1. God created two separate and equal persons.[1]

- They are equal in value.
- They are equal in their relationship with God.
- They are equal in their separateness from the rest of creation.
- They are equal in their authority.
- They are equal in their holdings.
- They are equal in their responsibility.

Now how did they get that way? God chose a very interesting method for creating the man and the woman and bonding them together in mutual dependence. First, the man is "formed"—that word is not used of any other creation. Man is not just suddenly here but is contemplated and artfully formed by God. He will be vested with the image and the likeness of God Himself. Also from this vested stock will come the woman. She will share not only the nature of the male, but the nature of God as well, thus establishing her value and relationship to both God and the man. Mankind, and only mankind, is alive by virtue of the breath of God. Into no other creature did God breathe life. He merely established their life process. But into man He breathed, establishing forever the unique tie between God and humans. No other creature competes—all others belong to man; but man does not belong to man—man belongs to God! Herein is our value; herein our identity and purpose. All other explanations of our purpose are foolish and hollow. It is not in our achievements that we find meaning—the achievements of one generation are scoffed at by the achievements of the next. No, it's that in our very being resides the animating breath of God! Here is the crowning wonder of our identity! Any form of humanism that leaves out God is but a mockery of man. It is in *God* that man is discovered and understood; anything less is blasphemous.

Fellowship Was in the Plan

Now God makes a very important statement in verse 18 of chapter 2: "It is not good for the man to be alone." This says many significant things about man. This is not a flaw in God's creation. God is not saying, "I have made a mistake. This poor fellow is going to be lonely so I'll give him a playmate." Remember, it is God's *intention* to create both male and female. The reason it is not good for the man to be alone is because he wasn't *intended* to be alone. He was created not to be alone. God's purpose for this whole creation is that it be ruled by both man and woman. This rule is so unflinching that in procreation there will be born both male and female and they will unite and leave the original family unit. They are to extend the rule over creation and enter into their inheritance through the establishment of families.

The next phrase is also important. God says, "I will make a helper suitable for him." Some have combined these words and come up with a strange word—*helpmeet*. After coining this word (it was originally *helpmate*)—the creators then wrote their own definition and built their theology of man and marriage.

What God is stating here is that He intentionally created the man dependent. He is first dependent upon God—for it is God's breath that animates him and defines his being. He is, furthermore, dependent upon another creature not yet in existence. This dependency is beautifully illustrated to the man when God gives him an assignment. I'll deal with that assignment in just a minute.

The word "suitable" is an important word. It means

to meet face to face; a helper who could look the man in the face; one who could stand fully with him, fully helping in every task. This was to be no slave or lower form of being. This was not some higher form from the animal kingdom—this would be a person, sharing the same nature—even sharing his very flesh.

Now the assignment. Before creating the woman, God shows the man in a graphic way that nothing else in creation will answer his need. He shows him further that the only solution will be found in one who shares his position with God and shares God's nature. There is only one source for such a creature—that is the God-breathed stock of Adam himself. After becoming fully acquainted with the animal kingdom through God's assignment of naming the animals (which, by the way, speaks of his immense intelligence), Adam is ready to understand the nature of his dependency. "But for Adam no suitable helper was found."

It is at this point the divine anesthetic is given, the rib is taken, the skin is closed and the woman made. (We use the term *rib* for simplicity in grammar. Some translations would put it "part of the man's side.")

Let me just say a word about God closing up the place where the flesh was opened. I assume that this would have in time healed naturally. However, it could have left a scar and a possible weakness. But it is not at the expense of the man that the woman is formed. God did not make Adam less in order to form Eve. She comes with no pain or scar to the man, thus with no guilt or inferiority. God had deposited in the man at his initial creation that which He intended to use in forming the woman. It is in this sense that the woman completes the man. She takes nothing from him—in her creation the man becomes what God intended, as does the woman.

Adam recognized this immediately. "This is now bone

of my bones and flesh of my flesh." (No mere animal—she shares my nature. She stands face to face with me. She is my equal in every sense!) Picking up where he left off before the anesthetic, Adam named her immediately. The Hebrew word used for man in Genesis 2:23 is the name he gave himself, *Ishi*; and when he beheld the woman, he said with delight, "*Ishah*!" It's as if he was exclaiming, "Great!—here's one like me! She shall be called Ishah—because I am Ishi. And this is no animal. This is not a monkey or a lion. This is bone of *my* bone and flesh of *my* flesh. She's me in another form—one I can enjoy and share the kingdom with."

After this description comes the statement that Jesus quoted in Mark 10:7, " 'For *this reason* a man will leave his father and mother and be united to his wife, and the two will become one flesh' " (italics added).

Naked and without Shame

Have you ever wondered about verse 25—"The man and his wife were both naked, and they felt no shame"? Usually in sermons that verse is separated from those preceding it as though it were a totally different subject. It is not, however, the introduction of a different subject; it is the culmination of this one—the subject of mutual dependency.

The man cannot declare, "I am sufficient in myself—I can make it alone." For the woman need only take his hand and touch the place where the skin had been closed up by God. Nor can she arrogantly declare, "I am independent—I need no one." For he need only take her hand and place it there. In the recognition of equal value and mutual dependency is found the basis of unity in a marriage. But that unity in marriage is declared not by touching the man's ribcage, but in the actual union again of a man and woman—the literal becoming of one flesh in the sexual act. From this supreme statement of dependency and understanding of each one's true nature and source comes the continuation of the human race. From this statement love is expressed and life is generated. Thus each person is an illustration of God's initial intention for the man and the woman as He established them with equal value and mutual dependency and gave them to each other. Indeed, the man and his wife were both naked and they felt no shame!

That shame came when God's purpose was despised and man became separated from God. The separation destroyed our understanding of our purpose and value. Instead of remaining the lovely and fitting statement of the man's dependency upon first, God and second, his wife, the sexual act became a means of exploitation. Domination rather than mutuality perverted it beyond recognition. The true understanding of sexual intercourse as a statement of value and dependency between husband and wife, and the two of them upon God, can only be discovered in the redemptive work of Christ. This redemption restores us to God and shows us again His purposes. It illuminates the terrible shame that has covered our understanding of person and the love of one another.

To once again be able to speak into the marriage relationship that they are naked and without shame is Christ's wedding gift to each godly marriage. Not just naked in the physical sense, but able to stand fully as they are—different, yet equal in every respect. These two can stand without embarrassment and without fear of domination.

Bible Verses to Study for This Chapter

Original intentions: Mark 10:2-10; Genesis 1:26-31; Genesis 2:1-25.

Regarding the intentions of God for marriage: Song of Songs; Matthew 19:2-11; Malachi 2:13-16; Hosea 2:14-20 (note v. 16 particularly).

In the use of the words translated "master" and "husband" there is a play on words that takes us back to the Garden of Eden. In the new love covenant that Gomer and Hosea would experience (a simile for Israel and Jehovah) Gomer would no longer have a master/slave relationship but a man/woman relationship. She would not call Hosea *lord* (*Baali* in Hebrew) but *husband* (*Ishi*)—my man, my partner, my beloved one. The *NASB* translates it "and it will come about in that day," declares the Lord, "that you will call Me Ishi and will no longer call Me Baali."

In Genesis 1 and 2 there is no *Baali* marriage. The word used for man in 2:23 is *Ishi*—that's what Adam named himself. When he met Eve he exclaimed, "She shall be called Ishah—one like me." "This is now bone of my bones and flesh of my flesh; she shall be called woman (*Ishah*) for she was taken out of man (*Ish*). (*Ish-Ishah* was the original marriage—a happy partnership).

It is in entering into this relationship that Gomer will respond as in the days of her youthful love. She will sing and enjoy her husband (v. 15). She will find a door of hope in the valley of trouble; a doorway leading to security, fruitfulness and peace coming from a relationship based on loving-kindness and faithfulness (v. 19).

The book of Hosea presents a picture of God's unconditional love for His people—a love which desires intimate, loyal, close relationship with them. He appeals to the original plan for marriage to portray the kind of relationship He desires. And in the process of writing this book, it appears He actually gave that kind of marriage to Hosea and Gomer—certainly a pair who had everything against them. If there ever was a woman who deserved to become a humble servant, just grateful to be married and supported, it was the faithless Gomer. Instead she received grace and forgiveness and a joyous, fulfilling marriage to a man who tenderly loved her!

Questions for Discussion

After reading Jesus' statements in Mark 10:2-10 and the Genesis accounts of creation, what do you think was God's original intention for marriage?

How do our immediate cultural ideas differ from God's original plans?

Were both sexes created in the image of God? Does one sex reflect His nature more than the other? What biblical reasons would you give for your answer?

Do you believe we were created in two sexes rather than one only for the purpose of procreation? Can you suggest any other reasons for man's creation as male and female?

Chapter 3/Jerry and Barbara

Who Messed Up the Plan?

What went wrong with marriage? It was all so perfect there in the garden, so innocent and lovely. What was "the fall of man" all about?

Some of the unfounded assumptions about these events lead to faulty theologies of marriage and of male and female personality traits. For example, it is often taught that Adam and Eve were in some state of intense innocence which made them incapable of determining right and wrong. (After all, if they could cavort around without clothes it must have been because they didn't know it was wrong!) There is something idyllic in the idea that they were mere children in grown-up bodies with no understanding of right and wrong. But such an idea makes Satan the means of enlightenment and maturity for this naive couple. This fantasy ignores the fact that Adam and Eve were endowed with capability to rule the entire creation and to stand responsible before God for their action. These were not naive children; they were God-ordained sovereigns. Furthermore, had there been no understanding of good and evil, there could have been no basis for giving the command not to eat of the tree; and certainly no basis for God to hold them responsible for their actions.

The tree was not the source for their knowledge of good and evil—God was that Source. The tree represented that point of obedience to the good which would secure forever their allegiance to God and their dependency on Him. When that point of obedience was forfeited the relationship was destroyed at its base. God could no longer trust man. All creation was jeopardized and made vulnerable to the anti-purposes of Satan, who himself had sought to be as God.

Together in Temptation

The act of disobedience was a shared act. They both agreed in the action. Some feel that Eve somehow tempted Adam and therefore became more guilty. But the only tempter in this story is Satan, who entered into a serpent and slandered God. Adam and Eve were the tempted. Neither of them was the tempter. They were in this thing together, both in the choice and the guilt.

"Now the serpent was more crafty than any of the wild animals the Lord God had made. He said to the woman, 'Did God really say, "You must not eat from any tree in the garden"?'

"The woman said to the serpent, 'We may eat fruit from the trees in the garden, but God did say, "You must not eat fruit from the tree that is in the middle of the garden, and you must not touch it, or you will die." '

" 'You will not surely die,' the serpent said to the woman. 'For God knows that when you eat of it your eyes will be opened, and you will be like God, knowing good and evil.' When the woman saw that the fruit of the tree was good for food and pleasing to the eye, and also desirable for gaining wisdom, she took some and ate it.

She also gave some to her husband, who was with her, and he ate it. Then the eyes of both of them were opened, and they realized they were naked; so they sewed fig leaves together and made coverings for themselves. Then the man and his wife heard the sound of the Lord God as he was walking in the garden in the cool of the day, and they hid from the Lord God among the trees of the garden.

"But the Lord God called to the man, 'Where are you?'

"He answered, 'I heard you in the garden, and I was afraid because I was naked; so I hid.'

"And he said, 'Who told you that you were naked? Have you eaten from the tree that I commanded you not to eat from?'

"The man said, 'The woman you put here with me—she gave me some fruit from the tree, and I ate it.'

"Then the Lord God said to the woman, 'What is this you have done?' The woman said, 'The serpent deceived me, and I ate' " (Gen. 3:1-13).

Look closely at verse 6. The last phrase says, "She also gave some to her husband, *who was with her*, and he ate it." The idea that Eve, being weak and vulnerable, should never have been out from under her husband's "covering" is unfounded. They were together. Satan addressed his remarks to Eve and she answered for both of them! Adam was right there with her. They both ate and "then the eyes of *both* of them were opened, and they realized they were naked . . . *they* sewed fig leaves together. . . ." This was an act of rebellion by two partners, both of whom experienced immediate effects of guilt and shame.

Their togetherness was remarkable: "The man and his wife heard the sound of the Lord God . . . they hid from the Lord God among the trees." As we read of

God's dealing with them an interesting thing becomes clear. Though their act was mutual and they stood together as partners in guilt, God dealt with them individually, illustrating their individual authority and responsibility before Him. God did not talk to Adam about Eve nor to Eve about Adam. *Because* of their equality before Him He dealt with them individually. Each was responsible for his own choice; neither was responsible before God for the other person. In our society we practice a simple rule of management: When dealing with a disciplinary situation you deal with the person most immediately responsible and he deals down the line. With Adam and Eve there is no "down the line"—they stand individually responsible before God, each answering for himself and each receiving his own judgment.

Separate in Responsibility

In my own walk on earth today, thousands of years later, I still must take responsibility for myself before God. My choices are my choices and I can't blame my wife for them. Nor can she escape responsibility for herself by claiming, "My husband made me do it." Women who claim exemption from responsibility simply because they are married need to take another look at Scripture. A husband is not the mediator between God and a woman. "There is one God and one mediator between God and men, the man Christ Jesus" (1 Tim. 2:5). Women who rationalize a lack of spiritual life by saying, "My husband just doesn't take spiritual leadership" will find themselves no less responsible before God. My imagination pictures God's end of the conversation to be, "Now, honey, just what does *that* have to do with it?!"

A theory related to this kind of rationalizing, however, is one that goes something like this: Yes, male and female were equal before the Fall, but after the Fall God established a new order. In this new order male was put in charge of things and female was asked to obey him. This is sometimes referred to as "God's order for the family." Since the female was responsible for bringing sin into the world she isn't going to be trusted with any more decisions. From now on males will make decisions. The female's punishment, in part, is the sorrow of having to obey the male's decisions.

That theory can be quickly dismissed by another look at Genesis 3. Had there been something in the Fall itself or on either the man's or the woman's part in the Fall that would have placed one over the other, this is the place Scripture would tell us. But it is not there. In fact, just the opposite is true. Their equality is so foundational that even after the Fall God does not violate it. Each is questioned and each tells the facts precisely as they were. There is no hedging, no excuse. Eve declares she was deceived and ate. Adam declares he was offered the fruit and took it and ate it. Both stand equally guilty before God, accepting responsibility for themselves.

God dealt first with the serpent. The serpent was not Satan but had been used by Satan because of the nature of its being. Along with the ground, this animal was cursed by God. Neither the man nor the woman was cursed by God. They were dealt with in an entirely different way, which again shows their separateness from the rest of creation.

In verse 15 Satan's judgment is announced. His final destruction will be accomplished through the woman. The person he chose to deceive is the very person through whom God chooses to establish a new kingdom. "And I will put enmity between you and the woman, and between your offspring and hers; he will crush your head, and you will strike his heel" (Gen. 3:15).

Consistently in Scripture the times that appear to be

Satan's points of victory have proven to be the points of his ultimate defeat. It is significant that the woman is named here as an instrument of God's redemption even before any words are spoken to her.

Now God addresses Himself to the woman. He does not address her through the man or through an intermediary. Because she is an equal partner in God's purposes she is addressed directly. God says to Eve, "I will greatly multiply thy sorrow and thy conception; in sorrow thou shalt bring forth children; and thy desire shall be to thy husband, and he shall rule over thee" (Gen. 3:16, *KJV*). That birth process which was to be the great illustration of dependency and love, that which was to be the shameless herald of God's intention for man, would fail to be the joyful experience God intended. Now Eve—and all mothers—will physically toil in bringing forth their children. The spectre of physical death is signaled in the very life process. Does this mean that God cursed all women with pain in birth? If so, isn't it ethically wrong (as believed in the Middle Ages) to attempt to alleviate that pain through anesthetics, education or childbirth preparation?

In her book, *Natural Childbirth and the Christian Family*, Helen Wessel points out that the Hebrew words used in Genesis 3:16 for pains ("sorrow" in *KJV*) is *itstsabon*, "I will greatly increase your [*itstsabon*] in childbearing," and *etseb*, "with [*etseb*] you will give birth to children." *Etseb* is used in many instances where physical pain is not inferred; for example in Proverbs 10:22 it is translated "trouble": "The blessing of the Lord brings wealth, and he adds no trouble [*etseb*] to it."[1]

In verse 17 God turns His attention to Adam: "Because you listened to your wife and ate from the tree about which I commanded you, 'You must not eat of it,' cursed is the ground because of you; through painful toil you will eat of it all the days of your life. It will produce thorns and thistles for you, and you will eat the plants of the field. By the sweat of your brow you will eat your food" (Gen. 3:17-19). Again we see the word *itstsabon* to describe Adam's "curse": "Through painful toil [*itstsabon*] you will eat of it." When the same word is used in both instances, why do some interpreters insist that women must experience pain in childbirth as a result of her "curse," but man's "curse" is only that he will have to work the field? The same word was used by God to describe to both Adam and Eve the result of their sin.

So the original words are translated as "anguish," "grief," "sorrow," "labor" or "painful toil," but the prevalent idea of excruciating physical pain during childbirth is not there. God did not give woman a special punishment of pain for her sin. The "curse of Eve" is nonexistent. The women of Bible days did not even know about the curse of Eve. Childbirth was desired, not feared. Mary and Joseph did not approach the birth of Jesus with fear of great pain, decreed by God as Mary's "penalty." The Bible of their day said nothing about painful childbearing; that emphasis was inserted much later by medieval celibates who believed in woman's intrinsic evil nature and her "curse."

Woman's joyous work in childbearing was mingled with sorrow; man, also, tilling a cursed ground would find his joy mingled with sorrow. But abnormal suffering in childbirth is not due to the "will of God" any more than abnormal muscle pain in a working man is "God's will."

The second part of verse 16 is, "Your desire will be for your husband, and he will rule over you." The mutuality that was such a declaration of purpose and unity now breaks down. For the first time, competition is mentioned. These are the effects of alienation. Dependency on God has been violated in the act of rebellion. Now dependency on each other has degenerated into a struggle for dominance. The word *teshuqua*, translated "desire," is a word which means "turning."

Teshuqua was translated *turning* in the Septuagint (285 B.C.) and also in nearly all versions up to 1400 A.D. Then, it seems, the monastic translators began to substitute words like *lust, appetite,* etc., in the section about Eve, believing the meaning to be that women were lustful, victims of their sexual appetites and, therefore, creatures who should be ruled firmly by their husbands. There recently has emerged some serious scholarship which questions these kinds of interpretations by translators. The Septuagint says, "Thou art turning away to thy husband and he will rule over thee."[2]

The emphasis is upon Eve's turning *from* God and reaching out to her husband. In her alienation she has lost the relationship which is her Source. Guilty and confused she turns and reaches out to her husband to be her source. She looks to him to meet the needs that only God can satisfy. She turns to grasp the man and the man retaliates and does what was never intended: *He rules over the woman.* This is the root of the problem of over-dependence—looking to someone apart from God to become our source. God warned Eve that her husband would take advantage of this and dominate her. But this was not a command or a necessity; both Adam and Eve could choose to turn and reach out to God rather than become over-dependent or possessive or grasping of each other. It was their sin that perverted their interdependence into over-dependence, their strength into competition; it was not the will of God nor the "curse." For God to say "He will rule over you" is not the same as saying "He *ought to* rule over you."

This competition between husband and wife now is passed on to the sons, Cain and Abel, who carry dominance to its final destination—murder—the ultimate act of domination. Thus the human race begins its downward plunge to chaos. It identifies its person by defining its lusts. God's intentions are lost, as are God's man and woman. The record is there for all to see:

- Polygamy violates the law of priority.
- Lust violates the law of dependence.
- Dominance violates the law of equality.
- The man indeed rules and the wife indeed turns from God to her husband.

Mutual Submission

But into this chaos and terror come the marvelous words of Christ: "But it was not this way from the beginning" (Matt. 19:8). In Ephesians Paul sets down a principle of mutual submission in marriage, a principle based on the way Christ loved the church. Husbands are told to love their wives as their own flesh, and wives are told to respect their husbands. Christianity breaks in with its liberating truth that in Christ both the man and the woman are redeemed back to God. The war with God is over and, therefore, the war between God's man and God's woman is over. They once again can stand face to face without shame or fear. There is again the possibility of equality without competition and mutual dependence without domination.

This restored man and woman are positioned to rule in His kingdom and together fulfill God's purpose for this earth. It is in the pursuit of that purpose that each person is defined and fulfilled.

God is glorified as we step into redemption in our marriages. If lost men and women can be redeemed back to God, then so can marriage! We can do more than pitifully mourn, "Look at the mess we made!" We can return to the original plan, finding the purposes and joys for which God planned the institution back in Eden.

In our journey back to find the original plan we will encounter—and refute—several erroneous principles that our culture and even our churches have fostered. In the following chapters we will deal with just a few of these principles and tell how we have resolved them in our own marriage.

Bible Verses to Study for This Chapter

Temptation and the Fall: Genesis 3:1-24; Ephesians 5:21-33.

Alienation from God: Romans 1:18-32; Ephesians 2:1-3.

Reconciliation to God: Romans 5:1-11; Romans 8:9-17; Colossians 1:13,14,19-23; Ephesians 2:4-22; 1 Corinthians 6:9-11.

Questions for Discussion

What do you think marriage would be like if mankind had never fallen?

What common marriage problems do you see as a result of men's and women's alienation from God? Which problems might we still have if neither were alienated from God or from each other?

A common example of the turning (teshuqua) in Genesis 3:16 might be that of the overpossessive wife who wants her husband's sole attention to the exclusion of his friends. What other examples of "teshuqua" do you notice as creating problems in a marriage? How could these be handled by a grasping partner who honestly wanted to begin turning back to God as his/her Source?

Suppose a woman believes she is under the "curse of Eve." How would this affect her understanding of her marriage and herself?

Addendum/Barbara

In this chapter Jerry portrayed the origins of marriage, laying a scriptural base for our thinking.

I would like to go on to talk personally a bit about one implication of what he's just said—namely the subject of strength. As often as I have listened to my husband preach about man's creation as male and female, you would think the implications of it would sink into my view of myself. But actually it is only recently that I began to see the discrepancy between the Bible's view of woman and my traditional notion of femininity.

Some of the following thoughts and verse represent my discoveries as I searched the Scriptures with my questions: One of the things I had to face was a conflict many Christian women are feeling: I feared the quality in me that I recognized as strength! You see, "strong" is not considered a feminine word. We associate it with loudmouthed, red-faced women who wield rolling pins and throw plates when angered. A woman who "comes on strong" is out to catch, dominate or control you. She is too forward, too frank, too harsh, or too brassy. In the office she's the person who readily gives her opinion—especially when you fail to ask for it! She's the wife who nags, the bossy school teacher, the matronly head of affairs in the local church. Her capabilities are great, but. . . .

So, I feared the quality in me that I recognized as strength. "Hold it down, Barbara," I said. "People won't like you; you'll become dominating, overbearing. Try to be weak! Pretend you are a soft, delicate, fragile flower; or like a "southern belle."

The Bible, though, doesn't categorize "strong" in a list of masculine words. It doesn't categorize other qualities as masculine or feminine either. In the Bible, personality qualities are godly or ungodly, but not masculine or feminine.

It says quite bluntly and without qualification: "Be strong and of good courage"; "And they that fear the Lord shall be strong and do exploits"; "He may strengthen you with power through his Spirit in your inner being."

Does this mean *me*?

Christian Strength

Not a strength that seeks to dominate
to control
to compete or
prove something

It doesn't work to *gain* identity
Rather
it flows out of a sense of identity
an inner feeling of uniqueness and
worth.

Not a strength that demands love;
it issues from *being* loved,

A strength that's felt as
indescribable sweetness
tenderness
a reaching out . . .

Unafraid to say
I love you.
Can I help?

Equally unafraid to say
I need you.
Can you help me?

It delights in giving
discovering another
accepting
forgiving . . .
enduring

With such strength I am willing to risk!
risk leadership
its perils, responsibilities
inevitable failures and
hurts
sorrows

So I will lead in full measure
never apologetically
("I am only a woman")
nor halfheartedly
But with forthrightness
Courage
Confidence

I will bear the consequence of my good decisions
and my bad ones.

People's opinions—
important
treacherous
fluctuating.
My strength will not rest on these.

It lies deep within me,
Challenged—but never vanquished.
He who gave it gives it still
in my moments of greatest weakness

His strength is mine Forever!

Strength and Emotions

It seems that what we label emotional weakness often is not weakness at all.

My tendency was to notice how strongly I could feel, then become frightened at the intensity of my emotions—as though the very power of that emotion could destroy me.

If I allowed myself to feel anger, what havoc would my anger wreak? Intense love? Intense joy? Strong confidence? (Is that faith or arrogance?) Sorrow, grief? Anxiety and restlessness? Negative! Or, are they? I once described myself as follows: "I may seem to be emotionally strong (never cry—seldom show emotion). Actually I am merely well-controlled—out of desperate necessity. My emotions are kept under lock lest they harm me or others. The truth is I am terribly weak and don't dare allow emotions to run rampant. Their force is like a rushing flood, and I can't risk drowning."

Now I see it differently:

The capacity for feeling so intensely
        Loving so much
                Joying so keenly
                        Generating enthusiasm—
Not a source of destruction,
        but a storehouse of power—
                Energizing and motivating.
These emotions do not drive me
        they are my response to life
                and my offering to God
                        for use in His service.

I am no longer afraid to be vulnerable
I want to be tenderhearted (able to be bruised).
Being tough, stoic, above feeling pain or rejection
That is not strength
    that's denying that I'm made in the image of
    God;
        He feels emotion!

So, perhaps I'm emotionally strong
    and have been all along.
Maybe strength in the inner core of me
    is channeled into emotional rivers
        that can bless with their overflow
            of joy,
                worship,
                    love,
                        and gratitude.

Strength and Personality

Jesus was a man of strong personality. Paul, Stephen, Peter—and then there was Mary and Martha, Abigail, Esther, Sara. Not to speak of women as fearless as Miriam, Deborah, Huldah, Prisca. These were not quiet, retiring ladies who never let their thoughts be known. They did not wait to respond to action . . . they created the action.

Mild personalities and quiet ones—
  I've envied them—
    Wished I could be that way!
      "Why was I born exuberant?"
        "Why do I have to *think* so much?"

"You must learn to be more passive,
            Barbara; a responder, not an initiator.

Women with strong personalities are not appreciated. And especially they are not loved!"

If strong personality denotes a person who is obnoxiously noticeable,
or commandeering,
egotistical or selfish,
Then of course it is ungodly.
But if we mean a personality that has substance
or strength of influence
or is the result of inner freedom,
then I want to be
a woman of strong personality.
Fully living her life to the glory of God.
Freely expressing the reflection of His image.

Bible Verses to Study for This Chapter

Is Strength Dominance? Domination: Mark 10:42; Submission: Ephesians 5:21; Philippians 2:1-8.

Rebuke or reproof: 1 Timothy 5:20; 2 Timothy 4:2; Titus 2:15; Proverbs 9:8; Galatians 6:1-5.

Giving: 1 John 3:17; Romans 12:13; 1 Thessalonians 2:7-9.

Receiving: Romans 16:2; Philippians 4:10-14,18.

Respect: Titus 2:3-5; Ephesians 5:33; Romans 12:10; 1 Peter 3:2,7.

Trust, Security: 1 John 4:18.

Serving: Galatians 5:13; 6:10; 1 Peter 4:10.

Accepting: Romans 14:1,13; 15:7.

Understanding: Romans 12:15; Colossians 3:12; 1 Peter 2:17; 3:7.

Unconditional love: Ephesians 5:1,25-33; 1 Corinthians 13; 1 Peter 4:8.

Companionship: 1 Peter 3:7; Proverbs 5:18.

Interdependence: Romans 12:3-8; 1 Corinthians 12:4-27; Ephesians 4:15,25.

Transparency, Self-disclosure: 1 John 1:6-10.

Encouraging: Hebrews 3:13; Ephesians 4:29; 1 Thessalonians 2:11.

Questions for Discussion

Many questions are posed in this chapter. Having read the entire chapter, what are some possible answers for:

Is strength dominance? Why or why not?

Can two equally strong people submit to each other? Marry each other? Will one or the other be forced to gain dominance in the relationship?

How do we handle disagreement in an attitude of submission? Differing tastes or opinions?

Is submission ever a matter of denying my own value or identity?

What are some possible causes when a good, warm, comfortable friendship starts to feel strained?

Notes

1. Helen Wessel, *Natural Childbirth and the Family* (New York: Harper and Row Publishers, Inc., 1974).
2. Carl F. Keil and Franz Delitzsch, *Pentateuch,* Old Testament Commentaries (Grand Rapids: Wm. B. Eerdmans Publishing Co., 1971), vol. 1, p. 112.

Chapter 4/Barbara

What About the Domination/Submission Principle?

Strength is often associated with dominance. We believe the weak are ruled by the strong; therefore, in every relationship, there must be a stronger to rule and a weaker to be ruled. Even after years of historical progress in concepts such as "all men are created equal" and "life, liberty and justice for all," we still tend to think that strength equals control, victory and power over another. There is a tendency to view authority in the church as spiritual control over people's lives—we even have religious terms to describe what really is domination.

If I am strong, will I then be dominant? Does it mean I will always lead and never follow? Can two equally strong people have a good friendship? Or work in harmony together? Should two strong people marry each other? If they do, will one be forced to gain dominance in the relationship?

Many Christians fail to realize that relationships of domination are forbidden in the Kingdom of God. But Jesus made a point of stressing this: " 'You know that those who are regarded as rulers of the Gentiles lord it over them, and their high officials exercise *authority over them. Not so with you.* Instead, whoever wants to become great among you must be your servant, and whoever wants to be first must be slave of all. For even the Son of Man did not come to be served, but to serve, and to give his life as a ransom for many' " (Mark 10:42-45, italics added).

In a relationship of total domination, the dominator does not really *care* about the other person. The question "What are *your* needs?" is not asked. The relationship exists to fulfill *my* needs; that's why my expectations are so important to me—I have no use for you if you fail to meet them. So my love is conditional: you are chosen as my friend (or partner) not because you have *value* to me or worth in yourself, but because you make me feel good or build up my image in the eyes of others or gratify my physical drives for warmth, food, touch or sex.

If I dominate, that becomes the motive for the whole relationship, so my stance toward your needs is one of indifference (unless I can use a "concern" for your needs as another tool in domination). If I cannot get you to meet my needs of your own accord, then as the dominator I will pass laws, set down ultimatums, appeal to your "scriptural" duties or sense of obligation.

This kind of "love" is a devouring, possessive, self-centered perversion. It places my self-gratification and happiness as the supreme goal. I then find it impossible to place the highest good of my beloved as the motivating force of my relationship to him or her.

In a sense, it seems there are two kinds of relationships possible in marriage—or between Christians who are friends, fellow workers or members of a group:

1. A relationship of mutual submission
2. A relationship of domination
    a. husband or person A dominates

b. wife or person B dominates
c. they take turns dominating

Many marriages are *c* marriages—power is traded back and forth, either by struggle or by mutual agreement: "You've been in control long enough; now it's my turn"; or, "You've made all the decisions this month, now I should make them for a while"; or "You had your way about the vacation, it seems I should have my way about the furniture."

Fairness is appealed to. And sometimes one partner fears that the other partner will leave if he or she isn't given power for a while. In some situations the balance of power may be deliberately divided; in others it is kept precariously intact like a seesaw. True, we can keep peace in the house this way. Some people call it "give and take"; others say marriage is a fifty-fifty proposition. This works for many people. They find a way to survive without war. But for the people of God something better is possible—something far more deeply satisfying.

Domination is not always overt. In many marriages a nagging, ill-tempered wife appears to run the family. In actuality the quiet, seemingly deaf husband simply ignores her and does what he wants. He guides the family by independent decisions which he simply announces without consultation.

In other families a tyrant-like husband regularly reminds the children that he is the head of the home. All agree, but his wife has learned to skillfully manipulate him on every decision. She rarely fails to get her way but has him convinced that he's the boss. It is this kind of subliminal domination that is referred to in the satirical cliché, "She who submits to a man will eventually rule him." Remember the Jewish mother in *Fiddler on the Roof*? Father would rage, in his lovable way, "And furthermore, I'm the head of this house! . . . Aren't I, Golda?" "Of course, dear!" she always replied.

Insecure people often control in another fashion. They control through their overdependence. The supposed leader in the relationship may at first feel benevolent, kind or motherly. This eventually degenerates into an inordinate sense of responsibility; the uncomfortable awareness that I'm being asked to carry a person who really should be walking!

On the other hand, in a relationship of submission we see two responsible adults interacting with respect and dignity. Each sees the true value of the other and relates on the basis of that value. Two important passages of Scripture define this as the way all Christians are to relate: "Submit to one another out of reverence for Christ" (Eph. 5:21). "If you have any encouragement from being united with Christ, if any comfort from his love, if any fellowship with the Spirit, if any tenderness and compassion, then make my joy complete by being like-minded, having the same love, being one in spirit and purpose. Do nothing out of selfish ambition or vain conceit, but in humility consider others better than yourselves. Each of you should look not only to your own interests, but also to the interests of others. Your attitude should be the same as that of Christ Jesus: Who, being in very nature God, did not consider equality with God something to be grasped, but made himself nothing, taking the very nature of a servant, being made in human likeness" (Phil. 2:1-7).

These Scripture verses hold up Jesus as our example of the attitude of submission—He who had the most reason of all to dominate and be served! He made Himself—voluntarily—a servant to His followers.

A submissive attitude considers your needs, goals and desires as important as my own. I show my love by listening to you, receiving you and what you say and feel; I am always ready to understand; I reach out and respond to you. I serve you. This attitude is the true opposite of selfishness and pride. What you want actually becomes important to me—even if it's only something like a new fishing pole, or time to enjoy your favorite hobby.

Submission Is Giving

In true submission I find joy in giving time or gifts—any tangible or intangible thing; there is no begrudging or dutiful giving. Nor do I give gifts to evoke a response or to place obligation on the receiver.

The joy of the gift is in the act of giving itself because of the value I place on the person I give to and the joy I find in expressing love to him. The same delight comes in giving understanding, comfort, affection, encouragement or support. It is not, "I'll sacrifice myself to give you these things because you're asking for them or hinting that you need them." It is not, "You make me feel that I *should* take time to give—so I'll sit down and listen (though I'd rather be doing something else)." Instead I learn that because we truly value each other we can care about each other's needs and choose to listen, understand, comfort or encourage.

In a relationship of submission I find joy in giving, in serving, in helping. I can lead and you can help with enthusiasm, gladly; and this can easily be reversed. In a relationship of domination I give out of condescending maternalism, paternalism, or to gain control. You give out of duty, compliance, obedience or fear. But in true submission there is the joy of giving as an end in itself—love is its own aim. In a relationship of submission, my question is, "What are your desires, your needs, and how can I serve you?" In one of domination my question is, "How can I get what I want from you? Here are my desires; how can I use you to fulfill them?"

In using words like *joy, delight* and *affection*, we do not mean to imply that this is a relationship based on emotions—quite the contrary! It is a relationship in which I act not out of my emotions, but out of my values. Joy is not my basic motivation; the *value* is. I make choices based upon the things I value. And when I really understand the value God places on you, it will cause me to value you highly. That value I place upon you will be the prime consideration when I make my choices, not my feelings of the moment. At times I may choose to give you comfort when I don't feel comforting, gentleness when I feel like shouting. I may give when I feel like grasping, talk when I feel like withdrawing, reach out to you when I'm terribly afraid.

Not always will my emotions coincide with my values, but my choices will coincide with my values. And sometimes those very choices will change my emotions. They may bring on feelings of warmth and joy that surprise me. And sometimes, too, the most loving thing I can do in respect for your value will be to share with you the emotions I'm feeling. But this is not because my emotions are the supreme value of this relationship—they are simply a portion of the person I bring as I come to share myself.

As we read earlier in Philippians 2, servanthood is a Christlike value. Jesus living in me will express Himself in serving you. So servanthood is also a value out of which I make choices. Sometimes I feel like serving you; other days I feel like pleasing myself. When I declare, "I want to serve you," I may not be expressing my emotional desires of the moment. Nevertheless I am expressing the true motive of my heart, the rational choice I am making. This is true integrity, acting out of my *values*.

Comparing these two kinds of relationships side by side may help to clarify the concepts. This is how I answer the question, "Is strength dominance?" If we truly understand biblical strength, we no longer have a desire to control or dominate in a relationship. Two strong people can give themselves to each other. Neither assumes an inferior or superior role but each takes the stance of Jesus in saying, "You are of priceless value; I gladly give myself to you!"

Submission Is Accepting

True submission does not deny my own value or negate our differences. It *offers* my ideas, opinions and strengths to you with the motive of adding something to you that only I can give; but this is an *offer*, not a command; a sharing, not a takeover; a giving of myself, not a power play.

In submitting to you I do not give up my true self; rather I give *out of* myself, not denying who I am but offering who I am as an act of love and trust. True submission cannot take place if I deny my true self because I then have nothing of substance to offer you—not a real person, only an empty shell.

Nor can true submission take place if I have not chosen to trust you. Other parts of this book discuss the development of trust in a relationship. But here it is important to ask, Do we submit to someone who is untrustworthy? Never! The Bible is full of warnings about this. Proverbs satirizes the fool who places trust in unproven people. Timothy and Titus were instructed to commit leadership *only* to tested, reliable, faithful persons. Misplaced trust is one of the most tragic results of a vertical concept of submission in the church, leading to blind obedience and misappropriation of power. A horizontal concept of submission takes into account the scriptural balances placed on leadership. Mutual submission can only exist when there is mutual trust. And trust is not blind; it grows out of knowledge. It is not mystical at all; it

SUBMISSION	DOMINATION
Ephesians 5:21; Philippians 2:1-8 *I allow you to be yourself.* Thus— I give up the desire or need to control you. I refuse to insist on trying to change you or get my own way.	Mark 10:42-45 *I force you to be like me, or be like my "ideal" or be controlled by me.*
Submission Involves:	*Domination Involves:*
giving and receiving	coercion
respect	exploitation
trust and security	manipulation
serving	obligation
total acceptance	intimidation
commitment	laws
understanding	expectations
encouragement	possessiveness
unconditional love	ownership
companionship	overdependence
transparency and openness	conditional "love"
self-disclosure	
responsiveness	
interdependence	
intimacy	

Figure 1

is a decision I come to as I am allowed to know you and understand who you are.

In the development of a friendship there comes a point when I know enough to make a choice. I have concluded, "This person is trustworthy; he will not harm me. I now choose to trust him." This then becomes a solid plank in the foundation of our relationship. Trust may be challenged by circumstances, questions, or even by failures (but who could ever earn trust if it was based on a lack of failure?)! To continue a relationship of any kind with you, I will again have to make a decision: "I choose to trust you," or "I choose not to trust you."

A very difficult decision, isn't it? But as a Christian I find hope in another question: "Can I trust the Jesus at work in this person?" Yes, I know him to be a weak human like myself; but I also know Jesus is Lord of his life, and I can trust his relationship with Christ.

Submission Is Encouraging

Biblical submission means I *accept* who you are! But it does not deny the necessity of *encouraging* you to grow or stretch or bring something into line; it still must allow room for loving reproof or rebuke. Although this may *seem* as if I am trying to change you, it is a valid, scriptural part of our relationship (see 1 Tim. 5:20; 2 Tim. 4:2; Titus 2:15; Prov. 9:8). Reproof or rebuke must take place in a framework of total acceptance and be offered in such a way that I do not intimidate, force or control your response.

In my encouragement relationship to you, the attitude of submission is one that will lend support to *your* ideas of what you want to become. It will not be encouragement to be what I want you to become. True encouragement has to do with restoring courage, not with changing you. When my courage is low and my confidence is faltering in the face of self-doubt, that's when a loving person can restore my courage by stepping in with support. Or when I declare my goals to you, such as, "I want to get through college" or "I want to lose 20 pounds," I have asked for encouragement from you. It is in order for you to give it to help me reach my own aspirations. Rebuke and reproof have a similar base in our relationships within the family of God. If you are doing something that, in my opinion, is damaging to you or to others, my place as your friend is not to come on like a fearsome prophet, "Thus saith the Lord, thou art going to hell!" But I have the right to simply share with you my feelings of concern, acknowledging that I may be misunderstanding where you're at, I may be misinformed—or even wrong. I offer my concern, not my judgment. I come not to condemn or threaten, but to encourage you to live as the godly person I know you to be.

Submission Acknowledges Disagreement

Christians often disagree not only on doctrinal matters but in everyday decisions. Even husbands and wives have different tastes, different opinions and political viewpoints. These can be enjoyable factors in a friendship if we know what to do with them.

In a relationship of submission I will seek to persuade, to convince or to make myself understood. In one of domination I will seek to force, to wield power over you, to coerce or intimidate. I will give orders or ultimatums or set down laws to be obeyed. I will use threats, demands, manipulation and play mind games. I show no respect for your freedom, dignity and value—only a desire to make you behave in the ways I want you to behave.

In a discussion about differing viewpoints, a person seeking control will be mainly concerned with changing your viewpoint to agree with his, to convert you or make you more like him. He can't be satisfied unless the conversation ends with your admission, "I was wrong. You are right." True sharing is impossible under these conditions.

It's a much different situation when I'm telling you what I think in an effort to share myself or to ask you to understand me. I can even say "I'm trying to persuade you—to sell you on my idea" in such a way that still leaves you free to retain a different view. This happens when I honestly respect you and totally accept you as you are. You don't have to change your opinion in order to earn my acceptance.

Submission Requires Communication

A relationship of mutual submission builds the qualities that make for rich and free fellowship in a marriage. But all relationships are not clear-cut cases of black or white, domination or submission. Often there's a drift from a strong, healthy relationship into a strange, uncertain territory I'll call no-man's-land (for lack of a better term). This relationship is characterized by feelings of uncertainty, uneasiness, suspicion or doubt. Perhaps a perfectly good marriage gradually begins to feel uncomfortable, unpredictable or insecure. In some marriages competition has entered, or one or both partners have become grasping or selfish. The symptom may take the form of arguments, insults or hostility. Some marriages may be in the throes of separateness, independence and isolation.

Figure 2 illustrates how this uneasy no-man's-land comes between the two columns of domination and submission. The arrows show how you may move, by sheer choice, into either domination or submission from a position in no-man's-land. Communication is the obvious means of transportation. Obvious, but not easy! We must

SUBMISSION	DOMINATION
Ephesians 5:21; Philippians 2:1-8 *I allow you to be yourself.* Thus— I give up the desire or need to control you. I refuse to insist on trying to change you or get my own way.	Mark 10:42-45 *I force you to be like me, or be like my "ideal" or be controlled by me.*

Submission Involves:	*No-Man's-Land*	*Domination Involves:*
giving and receiving	competition	coercion
respect	power struggle	exploitation
trust and security	grasping	manipulation
serving	fear	obligation
total acceptance	defensiveness	intimidation
commitment	uneasiness	laws
understanding	suspicion	expectations
encouragement	doubt	possessiveness
unconditional love	mistrust	ownership
companionship	insecurity	overdependence
transparency and openness	arguing and insults	conditional "love"
self-disclosure	ego, pride	
responsiveness	begrudging compliance	
interdependence	unpredictability	
intimacy	selfishness	
	resentment	
	separateness	
	hostility	
	independence	

Figure 2

each ask ourselves (and sometimes each other), Why am I feeling defensive? Is it self-induced or have I really been attacked? Why am I uneasy, struggling for power, protecting my ego—why do I feel a need to control?! Are my resentments real or imaginary? Are they the result of your denial of my value and worth—or am I just resentful because I didn't get my way about something?

Many marriage partners think they are communicating but actually each one is carrying on an independent monologue. True communication is based on dialogue—two people talking and *listening* to each other. In a monologue marriage the dominating person does the talking while the other appears to listen and agree (or pretend to agree). When one person in a relationship is unable to say what he thinks or feels he forces the other into a dominating position—often unfairly so. Dialogue demands risk; it is not always comfortable to say what I feel or think but it *is* the answer to the drift away from submission and intimacy.

To move from no-man's-land back to submission takes understanding, dialogue and—most of all—forgiveness! Because all too often we truly are guilty; we *did fail* to give understanding, to listen, to accept or love. Either I reacted hastily, or forgot to regard your feelings, or intentionally did something to tear you down. Commitment bowed to self-interest, or I wanted you to serve me rather than to serve. There's nothing to do but frankly say, "I was wrong! Please forgive me!" I remember writing:

Dear Jerry,

I need to ask your forgiveness
for hurting you,
making you feel unloved;

being hardhearted;
for my selfishness,
for failing to understand you and be
sensitive to your needs,
for years of misinterpreting
your words and actions,
for building walls to hide myself from you.
(I'm ashamed my ego was so delicate
that I
thought I had to keep it defended
against you.)
The list of my sins and failures
could go on and on;
but what's worse—
I can't even promise
I won't repeat them!
But I desperately need
you to forgive me
and not be bitter against me.

Love,
Barbara

As Jerry and I were in the process of coming to understand these concepts as elements which we each wanted in our relationship—but weren't sure the other did—we found ourselves completing conversations in writing.

Following are two samples of those conversations. I found the letter from Jerry attached to roses on the dining room table; I sent the second to Jerry at his office.

Dearest Barbara,

Your question the other night was interesting and a little disturbing. You ask what you have given me. I chose not to answer then, Barbara, because I wanted to write some specific things.

I suppose the answer could be made rather simplistic in terms of things—events—and experiences. That, however, is hardly more than surface. In approaching the answer I tried to conceive my life without your influence. I found I couldn't. My thought patterns, desires, aspirations, have all been impregnated with your presence. A person's value to another can hardly be computed by an inventory of items delivered. The impact of your person has in great measure created me. There is the unmistakable intertwining of persons which gives identity and value to each.

Without you, not only would I not exist as I am but there would be no Carmen, no Christi, or Jamie. I believe that would be a tragic loss!

The greatest thing—which is not other than children, but is illustrated by the children—is that you have given me someone to love.

I'm not sure you fully grasp the significance of this. For me (and I'm sure others, though I can only speak of myself), my needs are not so much to be loved as to be able to love another. It is in your receiving and enjoying my love that I am fulfilled. I don't love you so I can be fulfilled—that reduces to selfishness; it is rather that my need for a love object is very great. This is not nobility, it need not be described. I want you near me not so I can receive something from you so much as to have someone to express love to.

I am not now speaking of sexual love or of love-making. Those are important expressions within the broader perimeter of love but they are not the totality of the love (to swim in the ocean is not to perceive the totality of the ocean).

I will not pretend that I have always understood what I am now saying. I believe I am making an important discovery about myself and about my life. I am uncovering some reasons for certain feelings that have baffled me. Namely, feelings of frustration and even anger when a deep desire to express love through a simple act or even a lavish present was made somehow impossible; when you had a great desire for something—even slight or simple—but were hesitant to share it with me.

My dearest Barbara, how do I reflect on your question? What can I answer? Can you see that your willingness to be the sole object of my love—that in responding joyfully and honestly to my poor and often foolish efforts to love you—you have given me all I shall ever need or want, and infinitely more than I deserve.

I love you,
Jerry

Jerry:

If I am the object of your love
and you are the object of my love,
then we are each free
to be ourselves.

When secure in your love
I need not control you,
manipulate you,
compete with you
or remake you in my image.

I admire you,
accept you totally,
respect and trust you.
But I do not feel I must apologize
for not being like you,
for thinking different thoughts,
feeling different emotions,
enjoying something you don't
or being excited about
something
that bores you.

If I deny who I am,
I have nothing to give you
but a mindless china doll;
an empty shell who is not a
real woman,
but a toy you've outgrown.
When I share what I think
It is not to coerce—or
demand you agree.
I offer myself
to persuade—
encourage—
But—
not to dominate.

Whatever I share
is a gift of my love,

an act of trust that you'll accept me
and understand that
I'm making an offer,
an honest disclosure;
not a power play.

Love is not possible between superiors and inferiors
since the superior can only condescend
and the inferior only admire.

Mutual respect means I do not exploit
either your strengths
or your weaknesses,
but enjoy you
a unique friend.

To believe we can have a marriage of
sustained mutual respect
can only mean
we believe in forgiveness!

So when I ask, in the pattern of Jesus,
"What do you want?"
"What are your needs?"
I am not being subservient
nor am I giving my will to you
(handing over the lordship of my life . . .
even God will not take over my will)
I am rather
making a choice
a decision to love
to truly give—for the joy of it
because of your value to me.

Chapter 5/Barbara

Hasn't the Concept of Marriage Changed?

"Marriage is a piece of paper."

"Marriage is legalized sex."

"Marriage is the joining of two bodies."

"Marriage is the completion of your person."

"Marriage is a legal contract, with conditions specified by the culture in which you find yourself."

"Marriage is a sacrament."

"Marriage is a permanent, committed relationship between two persons."

"Marriage is living together with someone of the opposite sex."

"Marriage is the sharing of love and responsibility."

"Marriage is a sexual union"; (when you engage in coitus with someone, the two of you are considered "married" in the sight of God).

"Marriage is a private covenant between you and God."

"Marriage is a public contract."

"Marriage is one of several life-style options for persons wanting to experience sexual pleasure."

"Marriage is the legalized ownership of a woman by a man."

Each of these definitions of marriage has grounds for credibility. Depending on the set of assumptions you bring to this question, you could choose almost any one of these for a working definition of marriage and build a concept around that definition. But each of these, though possibly containing a part of the truth, has some serious deficiencies: it is incomplete, it is faulty, or it could describe many relationships other than true marriage. For example, "Marriage is a permanent, committed relationship between two persons" is the definition many homosexuals would like to see adopted in federal law. If that were our legal definition of marriage we would then need to redefine *home* and *family* and change patterns of legal responsibility for children, laws regarding divorce and property rights, etc.

Any definition of marriage that comes out of a cultural context is always up for grabs. We humans will define it to fit our needs and desires of the moment. So that brings up the question, If marriage was God's idea in the first place wouldn't He define the purposes and essence of it?

Human or Divine?

Did God establish marriage and then step back and deliberately leave it to us to carry on in any way that would best suit our changing cultures and environmental needs? Did He say, "Now I've made a man and a woman; they're capable of mating and bearing children, of loving, sharing, talking, laughing, building, planting, harvesting and achieving—either together or apart. I'll just back off and see what they make of the possibilities. Whatever they make, I'll call it marriage."

We simply can't accept that idea. Not only do some of us instinctively reject it, but God's Word tells us it can't be that way. Almost inseparable from the "definition" question are others: What is the purpose of marriage? *Why* is it? What was behind the creation of such a thing, if truly it was created by God rather than by humans? If God dreamed up the idea of marriage, what was it He wanted to accomplish through it? Did God plan marriage for man or man for marriage? Was it specifically to produce and rear children? Was it planned to be an end in itself, or was it a means to an end?

For example, some believe marriage was an afterthought which God had. Adam was lonely in the garden. He talked to the animals but they didn't talk back! So God heard his complaints and replied, "All right! You're lonely—I'll make you a helper. This isn't exactly how I wanted to do it, but since you're persistent, Adam. . . ."

Then, as some theologians seem to infer, God glanced down one day and saw the man and woman making love. "Horrors! How did this happen, Gabriel?! What have I done now!" So He established marriage.

A Lost Ideal?

In Genesis we can become very disturbed trying to define marriage. If it contained only the Creation chapters we could satisfy ourselves with a happy definition of male-female partnership. But then comes the story of the Fall, followed by God's announcement of the bitter results of Adam and Eve's choice—not only for mankind but also for marriage. The effects of the Fall are written on every page following Genesis 3. From then on we know we are seeing even in God's choice men—such as the patriarchs—marriage lived out as less than it was meant to be. We read of polygamy, of concubines, of women being bought and sold; wives being considered "property." Certainly David, Solomon, Jacob or even Abraham did not exemplify marriage as God intended.

The Genesis Creation story speaks of two persons knowing each other as friends, as well as sexually; two persons who have dominion over the earth together, a relationship with each other and with God. It implies closeness (cleaving) and a special commitment. But any casual reading of the Old Testament shows us the marriages of Israel were a far cry from this.

Nevertheless, the ideal was not lost. Malachi, Isaiah and Hosea speak of marriage as a covenant, the wife as a companion. The Song of Solomon describes a beautiful, godly love between a man and a woman—a delightful friendship of intimate sharing, play, devotion, mutual admiration and commitment. The prophet Hosea's picture of marriage is a masterpiece of artistry. Though clearly an analogy of God's love for faithless Israel, it communicates the high ideal of marriage as God planned it to be. The emphasis is on unconditional love that keeps reaching out, keeps believing, restoring, comforting, forgiving; this picture tells us something of God's concept of marriage. So does the analogy of the bride as a symbol of the church in Revelation. There the bride depicts the church and her relationship to Christ. The same symbol is used even more fully in Ephesians 5:32 where Paul says, "This is a profound mystery—but I am talking about Christ and the church."

Few human marriages, especially at the time Paul was writing, would qualify as a model for showing people how Jesus wanted to relate to His bride, the church. Of how many couples in Ephesus could He have said, "Now, you two—yes, Mary and John—stand up! I want people to see who you are. Now, folks, have you noticed how these two love each other? Do you see the unity they have, the caring and the closeness and respect? *That's* how I want to relate to all of you!"

To most Ephesian Christians it was a revolutionary

command when Paul said, "Husbands, *love* your wives." In Greek culture at that time few *wives* were loved. Mistresses were loved; wives were functional. Demosthenes explained the upper-class philosophy of love and marriage quite succinctly: "The hetarai we have for our pleasure, the concubines for the daily care of our bodies, and our wives so that we can have legitimate children and a true guardian of the house."

The *hetarai* (or mistresses) were the independent, unmarried women of cities like Ephesus and Corinth, often well educated and of high social standing. Wives were not educated and were considered a little less than persons—their status was below that of citizens, though slightly higher than slaves. Wives were encouraged to find sexual fulfillment in lesbian relationships and with male slaves. The renowned Socrates reflected a Greek attitude when he said, "I can think of no person to whom one talks less than his wife."

So Paul was appealing to a much higher ideal than the definition of marriage which his culture presented. And his description of that ideal has changed the definition itself. It has lifted our thinking about the purpose of marriage.

In the New Testament the Greek word used for marriage is *gameō*, which as a verb can mean "to marry," "to celebrate a wedding," or "to have sexual relations." As a noun, *gamos*, it can mean "a wedding," "marriage" (whether regarded as temporary or permanent), or "the wedding feast." *Gameō* is derived from the root word *gam* or *gem*, meaning "to fit together" or "pair." So, the Greek word for marriage did not in itself contain the complete biblical definition, though it did refer to the sexual union and "pairing" aspects of the original plan.

In Scripture there is no concept of marriage without sexual union—it can't be *merely* a permanent, committed relationship, for example. Neither does the scriptural definition allow for any other combination than male and female. Intercourse is implicit in the definition[1]. However, that can't be the *only* defining factor, because the Bible does not view sexual union in itself as marriage. Rape, for example, is not called marriage, nor is seduction or any other extramarital act. A valid marriage could not be had by living together, by private commitment or by any set of accidental circumstances. A secret marriage was impossible in the Old and New Testament because the very term would be a misnomer. In both Old and New Testament times marriage was a publicly declared choice, a covenant, a contract that was known by all. The consummation of a marriage was announced publicly at the point at which the couple were no longer "betrothed" but were "husband and wife." And, of course, this was the moment of celebration; the procession in which the groom and his friends went to the bride's home and brought her to the groom's home. After the bride was taken into the groom's chamber the feasting began. The marriage contract had been sealed; what had been a legal promise was now a real commitment. The covenant had been actualized—the two had become one flesh.

This was understood to be more than a legal contract and also more than a solemn promise. It was seen as a covenant with God—a personal commitment to God regarding the man's relationship with this one woman and her commitment to God regarding her relationship to this one man. Each was responsible to God for the way he/she kept the covenant. Any behavior that denied the value of the marriage partner or denied the one flesh reality of the relationship was considered a despising of the covenant, a breach of promise to God.

The Old Testament refers often to the idea that marriage is a covenant. In Ezekiel, for example, it is alluded to in one of the passages where God uses the analogy of marriage to express His relationship with His people. "I spread the corner of my garment over you and covered your nakedness. I gave you my solemn oath and entered into a covenant with you, declares the Sovereign Lord, and you became mine" (Ezek. 16:8).

The book of Malachi focuses on the issue of despising God's covenant. Specifically it emphasizes the seriousness of marriage as a covenant with God. "You ask, 'Why?' It is because the Lord is acting as the witness between you and the wife of your youth, because you have broken faith with her, though she is your partner, the wife of your marriage covenant. Has not the Lord made them one? In flesh and spirit they are his. And why one? Because he was seeking godly offspring. So guard yourself in your spirit, and do not break faith with the wife of your youth" (Mal. 2:14,15).

And Proverbs talks about the adulteress. "Who has left the partner of her youth and ignored the covenant she made before God" (Prov. 2:17).

Jesus Adds Understanding

In that framework of culture Jesus and the New Testament writers began talking about what God *really* wanted marriage to be. Jesus disturbed even the disciples when He said that marriage was supposed to be permanent. "If this is the situation between a husband and wife," they replied, "it would be better not to marry" (see Matt. 19:10).

Jesus didn't dispute that; in fact He went on to mention the validity of a single life-style for those who really felt they wanted it. But He explained that the law's provision for divorce was only because man, in his sin, was incapable of marriage as God had planned it. Forced to live with a woman he despised (due to the hardness of his heart) a man could become so abusive that divorce was at least a way of preventing murder! It was an escape hatch, given with legal boundaries, designed to protect a woman.

In this discussion Jesus said that God had originally planned marriage to be monogamous, for life, to include sexual union (one flesh) and also a cleaving together. To "cleave" means to establish a deep, personal attachment. The same word is used of Ruth and Naomi (see Ruth 1:14), of the people and King David, (see 2 Samuel 20:2), and eight times of Israel and Jehovah. The word is translated sometimes "adhere to" or "stick to." It implies a total lifetime commitment of two complete persons, not merely a sexual union or financial partnership or sharing of parenting responsibilities. Jesus restated the concept of "leaving father and mother" to do this, which tells us that marriage was to be the relationship of special choice, distinct from all others, valued even above our loyalty to parents.

The Apostles Build on Jesus' Teaching

Further along in the New Testament Peter insists that marriage is a relationship of partners ("heirs [together] of the gracious gift of life," 1 Pet. 3:7), of communication, mutual knowledge and understanding, mutual respect and honor. Husbands are to know their wives, understand them, and build them up.

In 1 Corinthians 7 Paul defines marriage as "belonging to another" (see v. 4). He emphasizes that the husband's body is now not only his but belongs to his wife; likewise the wife's body now belongs to the husband.

In the same chapter, however, Paul goes on to remind Christians that marriage is a temporal relationship. There is something even more important than this relationship at its best; that something is living for Christ, abiding in Him. For a Christian, that eternal relationship must always be valued as central to all of life. Our union with Jesus gives meaning and value to the marriage. It also transcends the marriage union.

Now, let me attempt to state in a few words what seems to be the biblical definition of marriage: *Marriage is a relationship in which a man and woman choose to join their lives in total commitment to each other permanently and unconditionally. They publicly declare this and agree to share each other's dreams, goals, work, play, joys, sorrows, children, responsibilities, achievements and failures. This relationship is based on mutual love, respect, fellowship, communication, loyalty and serving. The commitment is first declared in the act of sexual union and repeatedly restated and reinforced by that declaration. Once made, the commitment binds them together as one body in the sight of God, exclusively united to each other physically and emotionally, in a relationship of deep personal attachment that takes precedence over all other human relationships and is considered by God a covenant with Him.*

The question What is Marriage? was a very important one to me, one I felt I had to have a clear biblical answer for. Here's one of the many things I wrote my husband in an effort to explain what I was discovering in the Word relating to our experience. For a month or two Jerry had been feeling heavy pressure and discouragement but was not able to share it with me—partly out of his desire to protect me. I interpreted his preoccupation and distance as rejection. Out of the struggle to reach for each other came this insight into the meaning and definition of marriage:

I Need You

I need you in my times of strength
 and in my weakness;
I need you when you hurt
 as much as when I hurt.

There is no longer the choice
 as to what we will share.
We will either share all of life
 or be fractured persons.

I didn't marry you out of need
 or to *be* needed
We were not driven by instincts
 or emptiness;
We made a choice to love.

But I think something supernatural
 happens at the point of marriage commitment
 (or maybe it's actually *natural*).
A husband comes into existence;
 a wife is born.
He is a whole man
 before and after,
but at a point in time
 he becomes a man who also
 is a husband;
That is—a man who
 needs his wife.
She is a whole woman
 before and after.
But from now on
 she needs him.
She is herself
 but now also part of a new unit.

Maybe this is what it means
in saying,
"What *God* hath joined together."
Could it be He really does something
special at "I do"?
Something like His creation
of a mother when
a woman gives birth;
(something so real that
neither can quite survive
again without the other).
Joining together—in marriage—
two self-sufficient beings
into an interdependence so real
That when you hurt I hurt
(there's nothing I can do about it!).

Your despair is mine
even if you don't tell
me about it.
But when you do tell,
the sharing is easier for me;
(To know *why* I hurt, no matter
how frightening the cause,
is easier than living
with the theories
that fear suggests.).
And you also can then share
from my strength in
that weakness.

If we are one
then perhaps you don't always
carry the antibodies
within yourself

to fight every infection.
Some wounds are healed
by resources carried
in my part of our unit.

When part of a body is endangered
all the rest gears to its
defense.
Shouldn't that be true
in a pair
so committed
they are called
one flesh?

Bible Verses to Study for This Chapter

Marriage Defined: Can It Be Done? Genesis 2:1-25; Song of Songs; 1 Peter 3:7; 1 Corinthians 7:4.

Jesus' declaration: Matthew 19:3-11; Mark 10:2-11.

Marriage as a covenant: Malachi 2:13-16; Proverbs 2:17; Ezekiel 16:8.

The church as the Bride of Christ: Ephesians 5:25-32; Revelation 21:1-10.

Questions for Discussion

At the beginning of the chapter many short definitions of marriage are suggested. After reading the chapter discuss why each one fails to serve as a valid definition for a Christian. Why is it faulty (or incomplete) when thrown against Scripture?

What unscriptural concepts lie behind an agreement to have a sexually "open marriage" where each partner is free to have sex with others provided it is honestly communicated?

What is God's involvement in the marriage covenant?

Why do Christians believe marriage cannot be only a

private understanding between two persons?

Note

1. This doesn't necessarily imply, however, that a marriage is invalidated when impotence, accident or other factors make sexual union impossible.

Chapter 6/Barbara

Don't We Make Too Much Fuss over Sex?

The sexual side of marriage probably is overemphasized in our society. We have too many how-to-do-it manuals but, paradoxically, a lack of true understanding when it comes to the meaning of sexual love, the symbolism and communication involved in it, and the power it carries for strengthening and renewing the marriage covenant.

Sexual intercourse for humans is meant to involve more than procreation. It really can't be compared to the "birds and bees" for many reasons. Consider the choice factor—men and women are not helpless victims of instinct or of seasonal mating urges. Only man, of all creation, *chooses* when and where he will use his sexual drives. God planned our sexuality with potential for great creativity and growth. Within marriage it has limitless possibility for unity, love, emotional expression, communication, companionship and pleasure. But few couples tap the inherent potential in sex or, for that matter, in the whole of marriage.

At best, the sexual act can be an ultimate communication of commitment, an expression of love, a giving of oneself and a picture of true mutual submission. It can be an experience of artistic and aesthetic creativity, a communication of total acceptance, an experience of intimacy, ecstasy, self-forgetfulness and self-actualization.

At worst, it can be the joining of two bodies by people who are strangers—using each other—who don't relate to each other as persons or even as names or faces, but merely as functional objects for self-gratification. (The worst of this is usually considered rape, sadism, or child abuse, where one person uses another against his will, without the slightest respect for his dignity or personhood.)

Only slightly improved, however, are some forms of more legalized sexuality. Within Christian marriages there exist sexual relationships ranging from the sublime to the ridiculous. Ignorance or fear or technical misinformation may be the source of some of the problems. But even more basic than *information* is *understanding.* Sexual love is not a matter of mechanics; it is an expression tied to all dimensions of the relationship.

In a marriage where one or both partners are hardhearted, distracted with their own anxieties, indifferent, uncaring, not communicating, or questioning commitment, or where there is nonacceptance, fear, distrust or selfishness, sex inevitably is affected. It can no longer express the things it was created to communicate.

A woman who enters into a sexual relationship actually is saying, "I love you so intensely I want to give all that I am to you. I want to express my adoration, my delight in you, and my unreserved acceptance of all that you are—your body included . . . although your body is, in a sense, only a symbol to me of what you are and what you mean to me. My desire is not just for what you can give me in sensual pleasure, but it is a desire to pour out of myself, to give you pleasure. It is also a desire to know you in every possible way; my adoration of what I do know only makes me desire to know you more. The wanting to possess you is not a devouring, egotistical need to dominate, it's a sense of your preciousness, your supreme value to me."

For the woman there is awe and wonder and a feeling of great delight, even reverence, in beholding the body, the face and eyes of her lover (as in the Song of Songs). He is all that matters in that moment; nothing else seems remotely important. He is sweet beyond description; he is beautiful and she is honored to be able to give herself to him. In this sense there is the experience of transcendence, not because she has sought the experience for *herself* but because she is caught up in another.

Declaration of Belonging

A man and woman are saying *commitment* when they join their bodies together: "I am yours—this is a declaration of our unity. In uniting my body to yours I am declaring that I belong to you. You are making yourself mine, giving your very self to me. If you belong to me, you are mine to care for; you literally become my body."

This was what Paul was talking about when he said, "The wife's body does not belong to her alone but also to her husband. In the same way, the husband's body does not belong to him alone but also to his wife" (1 Cor. 7:4). This is why sexual union outside of marriage is so wrong. It is a lie, a breach of integrity. Two persons who give their bodies to each other without commitment are declaring a lie in full view of God. "I belong to you, but I don't belong to you"; "I take your body but I don't give myself"; "I want to use you but don't want to care for you"; "I commit myself to you totally—we are now one flesh (but I don't really mean it!)."

Outside marriage, sexual intercourse is a misrepresentation:

- I am joining my body with yours but I cannot join my life with yours.
- I will take your body but not your self.
- We are one flesh but not one in purpose or commitment or spirit.
- We will give and take pleasure but not responsibility.
- I want you but my independence also.
- I want to use you but do not want to be bothered with caring for you.
- I want to give myself to you, but can't give *all* of myself.

Love Is Not Lust

In God's plan intercourse is a declaration of commitment, not of lust. This is one of the major distinctions in a Christian concept of marriage. Lust, which simply means "over-desire" or "inordinate desire," did not exist when sex was created. It is a result of our fallenness. Lust is the desire to possess, own or control someone, for one's own pleasure. The Greek word *eros* denoted the same idea—the love that seeks to possess, the impulse to get what I want at any cost. Eros was considered the most powerful, most demonic of the gods. He could rule a man with unquenchable passion, make him the victim of his own overpowering desires, conquer him with a strange, seemingly god-sent obsession that drove him and dominated all his actions.

Under the influence of Eros a man could transcend his humanness, experience ecstasy, get outside himself into that other world where the gods themselves lived. Eros was sought as a religious experience, especially in the orgies of the Greek temples. This was the spirit-flesh world where a person could lose all rationality and become totally out of control, swept along by his passion.

So the desire to belong but not really belong to someone, to possess a person because "I must have her," or to "make love" because of the ecstasy it holds for *me*, often may have been how the Greeks looked at sex; but it never was the way God intended it.

If the word *eros* (or the concept it represented) did appear in the Bible, we would expect to find it most readily in the Song of Songs, which many commentators view as a book about "erotic" love showing that God does approve sexual fulfillment. But when the Hebrews translated that book into Greek in 285 B.C. (the Septuagint) they didn't use eros or derivatives of it even once. Love, lover, beloved—words like these are multitude in the book. But the word chosen to translate love in this book, along with the rest of the Septuagint, was *agape*, the love which chooses its object, seeks the highest good for that person, unconditionally commits itself to kindness and giving.

The Song of Songs describes sexual love very freely, but not as an expression of eros. It is clearly an expression of agape. The lovers are devoted to each other, enjoying each other, committed to give and belong and show mercy and kindness. Their longings, passion, and delights are totally human, unashamedly earthy, emotional and, at the same time, fully acceptable to God. This man and woman were full partners, friends as well as lovers; neither of them was a sex object in the relationship. Sex was the expression of their total devotion and commitment—the joyous celebration of their worship for one another.

Eros Versus Choice

In an eros concept of love, I cannot love you out of

choice; I am mastered by "fate"—I can't help myself. This emotion has taken me over and I am helpless to do anything about it. I must have you because my appetite craves you. I am helplessly "in love."

In his book, *Gateway to Heaven*, Sheldon Vanauken creates this conversation between a husband and wife who are reflecting on the disruption of their marriage: "Merely being in love with somebody is not a sanction for anything—but it *feels* like one. The very word 'sanction' suggests a sort of sacred approval—a divine okay. But being in love is *not* a sanction for the betrayal of anyone—your wife, your husband or your children. It's not a sanction for breaking your word or throwing honor in the dust. Not at all! But what's so important is this: in-loveness always seems to be a sanction. People don't expect it to. Maybe they mean to keep their vows. But then, as you put it, it *seems* so good and right. Like a god's sanction. The sanction of Eros! But it isn't!"

The dialogue goes on to discuss commitment.

"Commitment is a gift from one person to another. Its sole purpose is to give the other something to depend on. If a commitment ends when the one who gave it falls in love with somebody else, then it never meant anything in the first place. People in love stay together without commitment. Commitment is a gift requiring an act of will."[1]

Agape is so different from "in-loveness." Agape says: I deliberately choose you. I make a rational commitment knowing that emotion, delight and desire will rise and fall like the ocean tide. My commitment does not come and go with the unpredictable flow of emotions.

Commitment and Integrity

My commitment to you, no matter how great it feels, is only as good as my personal integrity. In fact, the degree of integrity determines the value of one person's commitment to another. Many people state worthless commitments; they declare intentions they fully mean to carry out but when the crunch is on, commitment is forgotten. It sounded good at the time but actually was worthless. A disagreement, an emotion (or lack of one), a doubt or fear—suddenly they feel released from the need to be loyal. "It would be hypocritical to keep this commitment since I no longer feel exactly as I felt when I stated it." So says the American mentality which places feelings in the seat of integrity. But the only reason to make a commitment is to give a gift that goes beyond feelings or circumstances and focuses on the *person*.

If that commitment is never challenged, never put to the test, then we don't really know whether it's made of words or reality. But when it is tested and holds firm, we see sometimes that we actually have more integrity than we knew. We find that loyalty grows under stress; it doesn't die. And when the choice is presented—Who will I love? You or my self-interest?—that choice is like a blaze of light illuminating my deepest motives, as a sheet of lightning in the dark night shows us a landscape we never knew was there!

Degrees of Love?

Individually we are not called to love the whole world. Only God has the omnipotence to accomplish that. Neither are we expected to love all persons in our little "worlds" equally; love is not a static substance we can measure out in cubic feet—three feet for you—three feet for you—oh, yes, I haven't forgotten, three feet for you also. Love is action—behavior toward the flesh-and-blood person I am with—and it is consistent loyalty to those specific people to whom I have willingly given myself. To some of these people, my commitment would extend to the point of death; I would die for them. To say

I would die for every brother or sister in the Body would be noble, but untrue! I am not that spiritual. I wouldn't offer to die for some anonymous person simply because he was valuable to God. Notice I say "offer" to die, referring not to a forced decision, but one I would make voluntarily! I would die for a person whom I had come to know and highly value, someone I considered dear, a person of significant closeness or influence.

John wrote, "This is how we know what love is: Jesus Christ laid down his life for us. And we ought to lay down our lives for our brothers" (1 John 3:16). Then he had to go on and tell those perfectly normal Christians (they really were made of the same dust as we) that they should stop loving only in words ("be warmed and fed") but begin loving in actual behavior. They really weren't ready to give their very lives in order that another could live; they still were learning to give of their food! Or money! My *life* is more precious than my food or money or my possessions. But in our selfish condition most of us still find it tough to give our possessions and money.

Jesus wasn't exaggerating when He said, "No one has *greater love* than the one who lays down his *life* for his friends." (see John 15:13, italics added). If there are degrees of loving, they are shown not in the intensity of emotions we feel or in the pleasure of a person's company, but in the amount of giving. What will I give to further your highest good? To what extent will I sacrifice my personal comfort and desires? This truly is what "laying down our lives" is all about—the how-can-I-meet-your-need base rather than the how-do-I-get-my-need-met base. It's the willingness to consider another and his needs and act.

My Own Body

When Paul challenged husbands to love their "wives,

just as Christ loved the church and gave himself up for her" (Eph. 5:25), he was describing a very high ideal. Perhaps he was describing a special degree of commitment—the actual degree of commitment that represented His idea of what marriage was supposed to be. To suggest *that* in a culture where the value of woman was less than the value of man was a very bold demand. If he said, "Wives are to love their husbands so much they would die for them," some wives might have demured a little, but others would have smiled assent. After all, you were supposed to die for your king; a citizen had to be ready (mentally at least) to give his life for his state. As sovereign a husband would expect that attitude from his subject, the wife. But Paul reversed the idea, turning the point of commitment to the husband. He is to value his wife as much as his own body because she actually is his own body—she is one with him.

In a choice between his wife and any other person a man's wife is his priority commitment. She is the one person he is to consider as valuable as himself. If there comes a question of choice even between the safety of another brother (or sister) and the safety of his wife, it already has been answered. He chose her in advance when he committed himself in marriage. The act of joining himself to her in sexual intercourse is a declaration to God and to society, "I have taken your body to become my body—we have become one flesh; I take responsibility for the care and safety of your body and your life from this point on. My attitude toward your body is exactly as my attitude toward my own: It will be nourished, protected, tenderly cared for and loved. It will not be neglected, or subjected to exposure, destructive habits or anything that would wreck or scar it. I will not build or comfort my body at the expense of yours. Your body is valuable to me, not because it is all of you, but because it represents you to me; it is the temple in which you live, and therefore it is precious to me."

The apostle Paul is saying that a wife is *more* than a functional object. He never teaches that a wife should keep herself trim and sexy simply because her chief role is to be an efficient sex object. He teaches a *mutual* care of each other, physically as well as spiritually. This is contrary to those viewpoints which see the body as material, therefore less valuable than "spirit." Paul does not denigrate the human body. He doesn't see it as worthless or as the source of evil. He repeatedly advocates the body as the temple of the Holy Spirit—temporary, but no less valuable simply because it is designed for this earth and not for heaven.

It is in this context that the Bible says we, the Body of Christ, are every bit as precious and valuable as the "Spirit" of Christ. We who voluntarily choose to be one with Him, who join ourselves in total covenant with Him, boldly declare our desire, "I want to belong to you forever; I give you all that I am." In this union with Him my commitment is a permanent choice; it is unconditional; it focuses on the Person of Jesus who loved me and gave Himself for me.

When a husband and wife come to the marriage bed with this understanding they have the possibility of experiencing the richest kinds of fulfillment and joy. As in their worship of the Lord Jesus, their worship of each other will grow in creative expression and depth. There will be times of sacred and solemn awe, times of rejoicing with fun and laughter, romantic moments of candlelight and music. The couple will enjoy nights of intense passion and, at other times, simply relax in a mellow glow of prolonged and sleepy lovemaking. When there is real understanding they will not institutionalize any one form of their worship as the "right way"—the perfect orgasm or "how it's done." To institutionalize is to make static something meant to be spontaneous; to agree on "the correct way" may seem to be a milestone or a diplomatic achievement, but can just as easily be the introduction of dead boredom. Sexual communication is creative, a growing experience of mutual worship. It goes through dry spells and highs and lows; at times it is a long conversation, at other times a short "I love you." In the great variety of beautiful things God has created for us, this is one of His loveliest symphonies. It uses every range of sound vibration; there is no musical note or chord that does not appear. The adagios are set between movements of scherzo and andantes; a listener who thinks he's heard the most thrilling crescendo is surprised to hear an even more thrilling crescendo later. This symphony, like Schubert's famous work, is unfinished. We who live out our abundant life in Jesus write it in our marriages in increasingly new harmonies. We celebrate His agape love to us; we celebrate our love and commitment to each other with continuing freshness and beauty.

Bible Verses to Study for This Chapter

Sexual love and commitment: 1 Corinthians 7:4; 1 John 3:16-18.

Sexual love as an expression of agape: Song of Songs.

Agape love defined: 1 Corinthians 13; Ephesians 5:25.

Paul's view of the body as the temple of the Holy Spirit: 1 Corinthians 6:12-20.

Sexual commitment and integrity: Proverbs 5:18-23; 6:23-35.

Questions for Discussion

Why would the Bible fail to agree with the idea that

marriage is simply legalized sex?

Why is it erroneous for a Christian married couple to view sex as an expression of lust? How would this view affect their way of relating in the non-sexual aspects of marriage?

What is the relationship between sexual commitment and personal integrity? Is it possible to retain integrity while pursuing sexual relations outside the marriage commitment?

Note

1. Sheldon Vanauken, *Gateway to Heaven: A Novel* (New York: Harper and Row Publishers, Inc., 1980).

Chapter 7/Barbara

Is It Wrong to Not Want to Be Married?

Is marriage for everybody? Why should I choose to marry? What advantages are there to getting married? Are there more advantages to marriage than there are to singleness?

Some of the reasons people give for getting married are:

- to share material goods
- to have convenient access to sex
- to produce children
- to meet the expectations of society
- to get a helper
- to secure a best friend
- to belong to someone
- to be known by another person
- to be cared for
- it was commanded by God
- it's necessary for success in my career
- to have someone to talk to
- to have someone to be with
- because this is the right person (the other half in Pla-

to's spherical man—I am incomplete without this other half of me)

- to give love
- to give myself to serve another
- to meet my needs
- to have someone to live for, to invest my life in
- to avoid fornication
- to escape loneliness
- to have a "ministry"

If a marriage relationship is a choice to love, as we have defined it, then why should we choose it? A man or woman can certainly survive without getting married. There are other choices we can make to love—such as the self-giving ministries exemplified by groups like the Jesuits, or by someone like Sister Theresa. Jesus Himself fulfilled His ministry and destiny without a marital partner. He taught (and lived) the concept that it wasn't necessary to be married to have a great ministry. It seems today, however, that many young people are taught to believe the opposite: "I must find a wife (husband)—then I can find the 'ministry' God has for me."

Two well-known preachers of New Testament days would have had to fight off matchmakers in some churches today. Can't you just see us welcoming the apostle Paul at the airport, "Oh, Paul, I'm so glad you've come; there's this terrific new lady in the church and I can't wait for you to meet her!" Or John the Baptist: "Now, John, you need to update your wardrobe a little. Camel skin is not in style this year. But I know some girls who would seriously consider you if you'd just try to look a little neater and maybe change your eating habits. I mean, who wants to cook locusts for breakfast?"

No, there is no scriptural indication that a man or woman must be married before he or she is worthy of finding a "ministry."

What other pressures are there for marriage?

Social or Cultural Pressures

Almost from the beginning people have married for social or cultural reasons. Old Testament Hebrews believed that marriage was for procreation, and that for the benefit of the husband. A man was to take a wife so that he could produce posterity, hopefully in large numbers. Based on this assumption, the patriarchs felt justified in taking more than one wife, especially if the first wife wasn't particularly fruitful. In many cases wives willingly cooperated in the rationale of polygamy and concubinage. After all, the purpose of marriage was not to have a relationship with the husband; it was to bear him children.

European history is filled with stories of political marriages. To the romantic American mind these seem like acts of cruelty; imagine the king of France giving his daughter to the prince of Spain for the crass purpose of strengthening their alliance! But the monarchs believed this was a perfectly logical purpose for marriage.

Sexual Fulfillment

If sexual fulfillment is a valid reason for marriage, then Christian couples who feel they may be sexually incompatible can believe that divorce is an ethical answer. And certainly the ethics of many ancient Greeks and Romans made perfect sense. With clear conscience the husband chose a slave girl for his temporary sexual partner (concubine) while a wife was ill or pregnant. This seemed acceptable to both the wife and husband. If sexual fulfillment is the purpose of marriage, then anything which prevents that fulfillment, whether temporary or permanent, would serve to invalidate the marriage.

To Become More Spiritual

Jesus never indicated that we should choose marriage because it will make us more spiritual, nor did He indicate that married people are more pleasing to God. And Paul, in 1 Corinthians 7, makes a strong case against the idea that marriage will help us have more impact for the kingdom of God or help us gain status or value in the Body of Christ; for that matter, says he, neither will singleness. These states of being are not commanded by God, neither are they more holy nor do they make us more valuable persons.

To Become Complete

Still prevalent in some Christian societies as well as secular ones is the idea that somewhere in the world is one special person who was created just for me—the perfect mate, the one who will complete me. "I need to find the other half of me so that I'll be whole."

In Greek philosophy Plato developed the idea of the spherical man. He believed that originally there was only one kind of being and a tragic event split that being in half. Greek mythology has stories and concepts built around that unfortunate god who then was doomed to wander forever in the universe, searching for his other half. So we today, as the legend goes, also can never be complete until we find our own exact, one-of-a-kind, made-to-order other half.

The problem with marrying someone who seems to complete you is that needs change. Both people will grow and change as they live together and it's inevitable that they will come to points in their relationship where they are no longer compatible ("She's not like she was when I married her!"); obviously if you're no longer compatible you simply can't stay married any longer! Currently incompatibility is the most obvious, most acceptable and easiest ground for divorce. Since you no longer meet my needs—obviously not the perfect other half I thought you were—it would be hypocrisy to stay married. I can't possibly love you. I made a mistake in thinking you were the "right one"—the person God made to complete me. I was misled; I thought I heard the voice of the Lord, but I was wrong. So now there's nothing to do but to be honest and undo this mistake so that I can again begin my search for the mate of my destiny—the real "other half" of me.

Is this a biblical concept, this "other half" idea? If so, then we can safely conclude that God has a perfect someone for me on this planet and I will know when that person comes along. All my empty spots will be filled by his/her personality, he/she will be strong where I am weak and I will experience total fulfillment in our togetherness. If this is not a biblical concept then we are amiss in teaching young people to "Wait for the *right* person. God has a perfect mate for you somewhere in this world."

Actually this pagan philosophy is contrary to Scripture. In Colossians 2:10 we are told that each of us is "complete in him [Christ]" (*KJV*). This concept of finding completeness through the mate of our destiny has done major damage in the Body of Christ. On this assumption too many people have entered hastily into marriage—marriages doomed to failure because the assumption was wrong. Single people often suffer subtle persecution in many churches where people subconsciously, or with complete awareness, believe he or she won't really be whole until married. They often marry someone too quickly in order to overcome this prejudice. Behind the tireless matchmaking of the married friends there lies an unspoken belief that he or she really is inferior until he or she is like them—married!

But rejoice, single person (as well as married ones)!

The Scriptures exhort: "See to it that no one takes you captive through hollow and deceptive philosophy, which depends on human tradition and the basic principles of this world rather than on Christ. For in Christ all the fullness of the Deity lives in bodily form, and *you have this fullness in Christ*" (Col. 2:8-10, italics added). The familiar King James version puts it, "And ye are complete in him."

Jesus is our Source—of everything! That is true for both married and single persons; to believe otherwise is idolatry, denying His Lordship. When any married person treats any single person who chooses not to marry as though he or she is incomplete, abnormal or spiritually inferior, it may be that person does not understand what it means to acknowledge Jesus as Lord.

For Fellowship

Having established that there is validity to singleness, as indicated by Jesus in Matthew 19 and Paul in 1 Corinthians 7, that we have a right to choose to be single and still be equal in the Body to those who are married, what should be the only reason for marriage? What reason will transcend cultures and the rise and fall of current value systems? What is the overarching reason for marriage that can be found in the whole revelation of the Bible?

Taking the Genesis account of the creation of man and woman and laying it alongside Jesus' strong words about the intentions of God, I believe we can come to a clear conclusion: *God planned marriage for the purpose of fellowship.* Marriage is a life-style of continuous, permanent sharing. I choose the word "fellowship" rather than "companionship" or "friendship" because I feel it is inclusive. The Greek word *koinonia* refers to the mutual sharing of Christians who truly love each other and express that love in a sharing of all aspects of life. Koinonia includes sharing both burdens and joys, material goods, spiritual growth; it also includes communication and understanding.

Marrying for fellowship—rather than to become complete, have a "ministry," experience sexual union, escape loneliness, for business or financial reasons, to meet expectations of society, to secure a helper or to have children—is the only valid reason for marriage. Even "falling in love" is not a good enough reason to get married. If "falling in love" is the determining factor in choosing to marry then "falling out of love" is a valid reason for divorce! *Falling* in love and *choosing* to love in a permanent life commitment are not necessarily the same things.

This is not to say that marriage is the ultimate in fellowship, or even a higher level of fellowship. As Paul indicated in 1 Corinthians 7, relationship with God is the ultimate in fellowship. As a Christian my reason for living is Jesus Christ—whether I am married or single. I choose to marry because the two of us want to share our lives and to live together for God. Rather than live for Him as separate units we choose to live in partnership, enjoying the kind of fellowship the marriage relationship alone can bring.

I would choose to marry because I want to give myself, my love and my friendship permanently to one person. Such a relationship then becomes all-important. Understanding, communicating and companionship with this person become more valuable to me than advantages the single life might hold for me; but still not more valuable than fellowship with Christ, which is at the very core of who I am as I come to this marriage choice.

If you are considering a choice of either singleness or marriage, this can give you some guidelines in making a good decision. Knowing that the reason for marrying is fellowship will definitely help with the question, "What kind of person do I want to marry?" Men should heed the warnings in Proverbs about contentious women who can make life miserable—so miserable you'd sleep on the rooftop rather than endure the nagging! And women should note the warnings in the same book about contentious men, angry and foolish men. What kind of person could you enjoy fellowshiping with for an entire lifetime?

When we become married, knowing the reason for our relationship gives cohesiveness to everything. It guides the way we plan our lives, the way we work and choose jobs. Understanding fellowship as the purpose of marriage is a key to setting goals in a home. It means relationship is all important; understanding, communicating and companionship become more valuable than financial success, than having all the household work done and the lawn perfectly manicured. Let me illustrate how it works out for us.

Togetherness Costs!

Jerry and I do not feel guilty about spending money to get time alone together. Sometimes it costs hotel bills or restaurant meals. That will not always be needed, but at the moment our four children and their contingents of friends fill the house; large though it is, we can seldom have an hour of uninterrupted togetherness!

This centrality of fellowship is one reason that I have an office at the church, run on my behalf by a highly capable secretary. When the areas of church ministry with which I am involved grew to the point of demanding full-time supervision, we determined it would have to be done in a way that left me still available to travel with Jerry or just to play a game of golf with him. We married to be together. Keeping that togetherness goal intact demands constant readjustment and flexibility. If Jerry and I viewed *ministry* or economic success as the purpose of marriage, our choices would be very different from those we are making now. Given our set of opportunities and limitations, we would do more things separately and leave less room for play and relaxing together.

This is true in different surroundings in each marriage. After services one Sunday I had prayer with a young nurse. She and her husband were positioned in good jobs but the two of them couldn't seem to work the same shift. They were frustrated trying to maintain a weekend marriage. He had talked to his employer to no avail. "Should I quit work?" she asked. We prayed about direction, about the salaries involved. I asked, "*Why* did you marry? To share life together or to earn money?" Susan and Bob talked about that and went again to the employers, explaining the importance they placed on fellowship without giving any ultimatums to the employers. The end result was that the employers understood and Bob's shift was changed. But during this time the two of them did a lot of thinking and decided they were willing to earn less money or to change jobs if needed. This was an important decision that may come into the picture again some day when other pressures bring up the question, "Why are we married?"

Singleness Is Not a Holding Pattern

If you are single and have not come to know a person with whom you would want permanent fellowship for the rest of your life, then don't marry yet. Fellowship with God, enjoy Him, come to know Him and become acquainted with yourself as a new creature in Christ. Fellowship with the wonderful brothers and sisters in your family—get to know many of them deeply, including those of the opposite sex.

Some feel it's dangerous to regard your singleness as

a permanent state, one you have chosen in order to better serve God. But the apostle Paul thought differently: "I would like you to be free from concern. An unmarried man is concerned about the Lord's affairs—how he can please the Lord. But a married man is concerned about the affairs of this world—how he can please his wife—and his interests are divided. An unmarried woman or virgin is concerned about the Lord's affairs. Her aim is to be devoted to the Lord in both body and spirit. But a married woman is concerned about the affairs of this world—how she can please her husband" (1 Cor. 7:32-34). I personally feel Paul is encouraging single persons to see the advantages they have in accomplishing things for God's kingdom. Whether I find myself at this moment married or single, I am to view it as a gift from God, something to enjoy and cherish. There are freedoms in the single life that cannot be enjoyed in marriage. I cannot, for example, pack my bags and take off for a two-year mission project in Africa. Exciting as it sounds, it is something I must deny myself. Not only would I violate my children in such a move, leaving them without a mother, I also would be breaking covenant with my husband. While I was single this was something I could do. When I became married I gave up the independence which gives that kind of easy mobility. The person who serves God wholeheartedly while single, enjoying all His good gifts, will also serve God wholeheartedly while married, enjoying other good gifts at the hand of the same Source. Contentment and fulfillment are not the result of either marriage or singleness. These are found in our relationship with Jesus.

Bible Verses to Study for This Chapter

Completeness in Christ: Colossians 2:8-10.

Singleness as a valid choice: Matthew 19:2-11;1 1 Corinthians 7:1-9,17-40.

Fellowship in marriage: 1 Peter 3:7,8; Genesis 2:18.

Questions for Discussion

From a biblical standpoint, what is true about these statements? Can you cite a passage of Scripture that contradicts the assumption behind the statement?

"I must find my other half so that I'll be a whole person."

"God will show me my true ministry in life after I am married."

"When I am married I will find fulfillment because then I'll have a reason to live."

"Larry has a lot of spiritual problems because he's a bachelor. He'll never be what God wants him to be until he finds a wife."

"All of Cindy's needs will be taken care of if she can get a husband to support her. It's just unnatural for a woman to try to make it on her own."

"I was in love with John and so I felt he must be the one God had for me. Now that we're unhappily married I see my father was right—I missed the will of God and married the wrong man. I've ruined my life forever."

Chapter 8/Jerry

Isn't Marriage Just Another Game We Play?

As Barbara began expressing her thoughts to me about the purpose for marriage I was stirred to ask questions about some basics of my own beliefs: What are the foundations of a Christian marriage—or of any good relationship?

Are some of us building marriages on foundations of sand? If so, the slightest stress will dissolve the marriage! Jesus talked about building our lives on a foundation of rock—namely the foundation of His teachings. This includes that part of our lives we call marriage. The foundation upon which a relationship rests will determine the strength of the relationship. Let me illustrate.

Dan and Jenny were an average young couple who married and formed a family. Dan had always been authoritative and independent in his manner. Those were qualities which Jenny perceived as strength; qualities she found attractive and admirable. She felt Dan to be a person she could trust for direction and security. Quite naturally, Dan assumed a paternal and authoritarian position in the marriage. That paternalism became part of the foundation of their relationship.

But Jenny was also a strong person. In addition she was intelligent and motivated. These were qualities that attracted Dan. But Jenny had been taught that her husband was to be pleased and kept happy even to the sacrifice of her desires. Because of her deep love for Dan she had no problem giving herself to the goal of his happiness and success. So both Jenny's abilities and the sacrificial stifling of those abilities became part of the foundation of the marriage.

The assumptions each made about the relationship also became part of the foundation. Because Jenny was passive, agreeable, cooperative and loyal Dan assumed she liked his paternal and authoritative ways of leading. Not aware of her sacrificial commitment to his happiness, he saw her passive behavior as a signal that everything was OK. He knew she was a strong and opinionated person, so when she offered little objection to his decisions he was convinced that he was the superb young husband he deeply desired to be.

Jenny assumed that because Dan was so happy in his role, she must keep him happy at all costs. She added to the foundation of the relationship the assumption that she must never assert herself or show strength. She certainly must not express her own views or develop individual capabilities. As children were added this foundation was instilled in them also.

As the relationship continued, overlaid by years of building on this foundation, certain flaws began to develop. Dan became more and more uncomfortable with a growing role of "monarch" in his home. The children began to relate in the patterns that reinforced the faulty foundations. Added to Dan's growing uneasiness and loneliness in this role was the traditional religious teaching that the husband must be the total authority in the home. This complicated the situation. It was no longer a simple matter of marriage—but there now was introduced a "spiritual" principle which was inviolate.

The Great Inversion

Since both Dan and Jenny deeply loved each other, they assumed the basis of their love was their relationship. The "Great Inversion" began to take place. It was so subtle, so gradual and seemed so natural that neither Dan nor Jenny saw it in time (some couples never see it at all). It is this "Great Inversion" that is either the seed of inevitable destruction or the key to the release of new and fresh love. Let's look at it further.

When Dan and Jenny first met it was *love* that was foundational to the relationship. Their desire to become husband and wife was a result of the wonderful awareness that they had found each other. They did not want to live absent from each other for the rest of their lives.

Now that foundation is inverted. They now assume that the basis of their love is the *relationship*. If they tamper with the relationship they run the risk of destroying the love. This very neatly locks both Dan and Jenny into a relationship built on wrong assumptions and weak foundations. Commitment now transfers from the persons to the relationship and "we have to make the marriage work" for the sake of the kids or the relatives or the church or some other such external entity—something which was not even present at the beginning. Both people feel trapped and strangely separate.

This case history illustrates how wrong assumptions can help construct a faulty foundation for marriage. The obvious solution should be, "Don't have a faulty foundation and don't make wrong assumptions." However, the problem is not solved that easily. Everyone makes wrong assumptions in a relationship. We cannot help but do so.

We move from two different worlds into sharing a life together. We may speak the same language but we come from different worlds. The terms *love, husband, wife, home, family, father, mother* are all common enough English. But when transferred into marriage they are loaded with emotion, nostalgia, fear and memories. Two persons may say to each other, "I love you. I want you to be my husband/wife. I want us to have a home and family. I want you to be the father/mother of my children." However, having said these words they, in all probability, have said totally different things. Those phrases and commitments call forth very diverse images in each of their minds. They each may be deeply committed to a family or love or home without being committed to the same things at all. But neither of them has discovered the difference and each is assuming the other is in perfect agreement and understanding. Each has very logical, though faulty, assumptions about the other.

It's not surprising that one conclusion people are coming to is to form no lasting relationships at all. Living together without commitment is becoming more accepted. "Open marriages" and other forms of love without responsibility are proposed as solutions. Ultimately, however, any attempt to have the benefits of marriage apart from long-term commitment is selfish. It is also destructive for those involved and destructive to our culture.

The call to the single life is also most attractive; but singleness due to fear of relationship or fear of the responsibility of commitment is a destructive choice. This is wrongly motivated singleness. In the long run, to be committed to oneself and one's own needs, desires and comfort is as destructive as being committed to a relationship based on a faulty foundation.

The values of society are always in flux, shifting like

driven sand. So our society is not the place where we can find these principles of solid foundation for marriage. The lasting source for true foundation is God's Word. It is there we find the solid rock truths that can replace our faulty assumptions. A life together built on the rock of God's Word will not fall apart in a storm. Adversity will only serve to strengthen this marriage; tension and stress will only increase the commitment.

The Form or the Person?

Now let's go back to Dan and Jenny. Since Jenny is committed to Dan's happiness rather than to Dan (she would never admit this; she thinks the two are identical) she analyzes his every action and reaction in order to make him happy. To fulfill this role Jenny has to sacrifice many of her ambitions and desires, even her person. This personality change takes away the very qualities that attracted Dan to her in the first place. It was her strengths, individuality and confidence that provided the magnetic field into which he willingly stepped.

And Jenny is not getting a true reading from Dan. He is playing the role dictated by his assumption of paternalism. He is becoming very unfulfilled and frustrated as he feels the loneliness of the "monarchy." When he shows this frustration, Jenny translates it as failure on her part to make Dan happy. She assumes *she* is the reason for his unhappiness; she must try harder to please him, must be more agreeable, more patient and indulgent of his wants. She refrains from any attempts to make herself known as a person.

At this point another stream begins to enter that convinces Dan of his failure as a husband. Jenny, in struggling for survival as a person, cultivates some friendships in which she can be herself. This seems like good therapy. However, it causes Jenny to dichotomize her person. She is one person with Dan and another person with her friends. She is not able to be this real self in her home with her husband—his happiness depends on her passivity. Dan observes all this and, without understanding why, he begins to resent her friends, responds in the normal authoritarian way, and disaster casts its shadow over everything—as Jenny retreats further from him.

Now there are two persons committed to a relationship pattern that is destructive. But since they are convinced that the basis of their love is this relationship, they are hopelessly lost to each other. Loyalty to the *form* of the relationship rather than to the *person* is the death seed. When my love is based on my relationship rather than my relationship being based on love, I am locked into inevitable unhappiness. Mere living and growing will produce enough stress to break that relationship!

But here's an important question. "Can this love between these persons be transferred to a totally different relational base? Can we attack the foundations of the relationship without destroying the persons or their love?" If we can, there is hope.

There are many routes that lead to the "Great Inversion" of love and form. Whatever the route, if the question can be answered, love once again can be focused and released and all the Dans and Jennys can be recovered. Barbara and I now know the answer is yes. Our personalities or forms did not parallel those of Dan and Jenny exactly, but some of our frustrations were similar. It was in a state of mingled emotions that Barb wrote the following prayer:

Frustration! and Hope

Jerry, what a magnificent man!
How awesome that he should have chosen me
and still chooses me.

How often I've thought
that I love this man
but hate our relationship
and wondered how that could be
knowing I'm committed to him
and care more about his life
than about my own.

How can I fail so miserably
to know him—
and let him know me?

I have so much to offer him
if I could find a way to give it:
My energy—vitality—my optimism
that seems to rise like a tower
of faith
when crisis strikes

I can be fun,
refreshing, alive,
shockingly (to me anyway)
loving, tender, comforting.
What it could mean to him
if I could ever be truly me;
if he could experience the
full power of my emotions,
my personality
and strength.

If I could even share my intellect
with its disturbing questions
and endless curiosity;
If I could learn to share it

without intimidating
or causing defensiveness,
without sounding like I'm
attacking!

If he could truly experience me,
we would have a romantic relationship
far beyond description
because I am romantic.

He is romantic too;
That's why I married him.
His idealism, his love of beauty
and adventure,
the tender way he has of caring for me,
the emotional content of his poems
and cards and gifts.

He is starting to feel
more and more often.
He is not always joyous, mellow
or passionate though.
(But who is ? Always!)
The rebirth of emotion went through many
waves of high and low
before it could stabilize.

What will be the end of all this?
I think we're growing, Lord,
in spurts at times,
and sometimes separately.
But it isn't all as negative as I sound.

My hope is not in my ability
but in Your power at work in me.

Questions for Discussion

In this chapter Dan and Jenny illustrate how people can build their marriage on a foundation made of wrong assumptions. Can you name some incorrect assumptions you used to hold about marriage or about the opposite sex?

What are some possible effects of paternalism in a marriage? Maternalism?

Which is more valuable in a marriage, the persons or the relationship?

Women are often exhorted, "Stand behind your man." What does this mean to a wife? To a husband? Can it be reversed, "Stand behind your woman"?

Am I expressing true love for a person by withholding myself, my desires and thoughts (as Jenny believed)?

Can I authentically love you by denying who I am? In His sacrificial love for us did Jesus ever lose His own identity? (See John 18:37.) If I, as a Christian, choose to lay down my life for a loved one, am I then denying my own value or annihilating myself? (Scriptures such as Mark 8:34,35 and 1 John 3:16-18 may help in thinking about these questions.)

Chapter 9

How Can I Be Married and Still Be My Own Person?/Jerry

Now, back to our question about foundations. If there is any possibility of reworking the foundations of a relationship—returning it to a base of love from which new relationship is released—we must know what God intended for the persons involved. Why did He make them the way He did? Indeed, *how* did He make them? Is it possible to bring two persons together in such a way that the relationship developing around them is simply the expression of their love? And if this is possible, how do we keep this relationship from imposing its form again and leading them out of their love to the brink of another "Great Inversion"?

Again we must go back to asking, What does God intend? Any discussion of relationships that leaves God out will be shortsighted. Our relationship with God determines our ability to relate to another person. If we are alienated from God we bring this alienation into every other relationship. On the other hand, if we open ourselves to God and respond to His love we have walked through the gate into new life. This new life flows into every relationship. I am loved by God; now I can love you!

Fulfillment for Jamie

We have four children. At the time I am writing this our girls are teenagers and our sons are ages five and three, respectively named Jamie and Sundar. (Yes, that is an Indian name. He is our one imported child. The others are homemade.)

Not long ago, Jamie came to the end of a frustrating day. He was unhappy with the world and disgusted with his home. He announced that he wanted us to move to another house. Barbara tucked him into bed with an attempt at comfort, "Things will look better in the morning, Jamie."

But things were not better in the morning. Jamie had devised a plan of his own, "I'm going to run away." He announced that he and Sundar were taking our dog, Gretel, and getting their own apartment. Well, Barbara of course asked the normal questions, "Who will take care of you? What will you eat? . . ." and she was assured that Gretel could handle all the parental duties. Gretel's huge German shepherd tail thumped approval on the floor, and the matter was settled.

Now Barb and I had occasionally entertained the idea of getting our own apartment so we could play the stereo as loud as we wanted and come in as late as we wanted, but this announcement by Jamie was a bit surprising. "Why do you want your own apartment?" Barb finally asked. The answer was perfectly sensible, "A guy's got to be hisself, Mom!" he announced and put on his coat to leave for preschool.

You will be comforted to know that he did not move out. The whole thing was resolved at school. When Mom picked him up, he announced that he had prayed to

Jesus and had decided not to move after all. He would miss his swing and his yard—and most of all—getting to go to Grandma's house!

It's a pretty basic need: "A guy's got to be hisself!" and "a gal's got to be herself." Such facts of personal rights are declared everywhere in our advertising and our music. They are declared from pulpits and literature in the name of Christian rights.

The difficulty arises when two people each trying only to be "hisself" try to have a deep relationship, whether friendship or marriage. These persons are headed for pain and heartache, to say nothing of loneliness. To make self-fulfillment the goal of a relationship will reduce the relationship to selfishness. Preoccupation with self causes the relationship to become parasitic. In order to get fulfilled, one or the other will seek to dominate—or be dominated. The roleplay of superior and inferior is worked out and the two persons become lost in self-serving.

We seem bombarded with the idea that the highest calling for a person is to find fulfillment. The Bible says something different: "If anyone would come after me, he must deny himself and take up his cross and follow me. For whoever wants to save his life will lose it, but whoever loses his life for me will find it" (Matt. 16:24,25). "I have been crucified with Christ and I no longer live, but Christ lives in me" (Gal. 2:20).

The words *deny, lose* and *crucify* are not words common to our vocabularies. The reason is clear. We tend to be the product of a system that believes the highest purpose of man is to glorify man. However, this is not true.

Where Is Fulfillment Found?

The creeds and Scriptures declare that man's highest purpose is to glorify God and enjoy Him forever. It is in the pursuit of this intention that we are fulfilled. To *pursue* fulfillment is to reduce all our existence to selfishness. But to serve God is to *find* identity and fulfillment. One attitude makes fulfillment the end. The other attitude makes fulfillment a serendipity—something we discover along the way to a higher purpose.

Now in a relationship between two persons it makes a great deal of difference which attitude we choose. Are we using each other to gain satisfaction or are we together designing our lives to glorify God? If we are seeking fulfillment in the name of love, then love becomes defined by the degree of fulfillment I am feeling. If when I say to my wife, "I love you," I really mean, "You are fulfilling me," then I have made a dramatically selfish statement couched in noble words.

A husband came to me one day and announced bluntly, "I no longer love my wife." I asked John why he had come to this conclusion. He shared with me that they had been married 20 years, that he had been fulfilled and so had she. However, recently the feelings just weren't there. He was bored with her and their family and their life and he wanted out.

After listening to his story for some time I asked, "Does your wife cook your meals? Does she wash clothes, care for the kids, etc.?" To all of this he answered, "Yes, Sally is a good wife." I said, "Then what you are saying to me is that in the past when you said to your wife, 'I love you,' what you really were saying was, 'You make me feel good and you make me not feel bored.' "

He discovered that marriage had simply been a means to an end for him—a way to get fulfilled. Now his needs were changing and she wasn't meeting them as he thought she should. So the feelings that he was missing weren't feelings of love at all. He was missing his selfish feelings of having all his needs met by a wife whose job it was to see that he was fulfilled in every way.

Christian Marriage Is Not Based on Mutual Fulfillment

A relationship based on mutual fulfillment will always taper off and the individuals will always want out—only to go into a more intense search for fulfillment and more heightened pain and failure with someone else. There has to be a clear understanding that we were not created for ourselves but for God. Any effort to find value and meaning outside God will reduce to selfishness.

In an authoritarian concept of marriage, fulfillment of the dominant person becomes the goal for both. Remember Dan and Jenny? The advice Jenny received about living to please her husband essentially placed Dan's fulfillment as the goal of the marriage. He became dominant, and everyone else, including the children, sought his fulfillment—to his near destruction. Seldom is this fulfillment seen in selfish terms. It is "for the job" or "for the ministry." Some marriages are based on the idea that the wife's vocation in life is to make the husband a success. This is not a Christian concept. It has, however, been Christianized and popularized to the destruction of many husbands and wives who, as empty shells, are hanging on to the cocoon of a marriage for the sake of appearance. As with Dan and Jenny, the persons are lost, emasculated; only the form remains.

So we are saying that fulfillment is not an adequate foundation on which to build a marriage. But we also believe that a growing Christian marriage *is a fulfilling experience*. Fulfillment is not the foundation for biblical marriage, but it is a very good word to describe some of the joys of it. When we feel "fulfilled" those feelings usually relate to having our needs met. But there are many occasions when my wife may fail to meet my needs, and many when I will fail to meet hers. There can be whole months—perhaps more—when illness or change, pressure of business or separation make it impossible for one person to meet the needs of the other. A marriage commitment will endure through those times because there are stronger foundations possible to us than the changing tide of self-fulfillment.

Those stronger foundations have been discussed all through this book in various ways. Before we go on to list them specifically, we need to share a little more of how the process of changing foundations has taken place for us. God doesn't just show us we have built on a foundation of sand and then leave us in our crumbling house. He teaches us how to replace the sand with solid rock.

Bible Verses to Study for This Chapter

Self-fulfillment: Mark 8:34,35; Galatians 2:20.

These passages develop the idea that, for a Christian, self-fulfillment is not the goal for living: 1 Corinthians 13:5; Philippians 2:1-8; Romans 12:10; 15:2; 2 Corinthians 8:9; 1 Peter 2:16-25.

Questions for Discussion

Why is self-fulfillment a faulty foundation on which to build a marriage?

What is the difference in saying, "I love you" and saying, "You fulfill me"?

If you are married can you identify the present foundations of your marriage? Are some of them weak or causing stress? Do your foundations need strengthening? Can you name things that could be added to build a stronger base for your marriage?

Chapter 10/Barbara

Emotions and Sharing

One Saturday morning I sat writing at the dining room table, occasionally glancing outside to watch the sunshine on the meadow across the street. It was a beautiful morning and I felt emotional; for the first time in months my emotions toward my husband were positive and hopeful. Some things were coming clear to me and I wanted him to know what I felt.

Jerry was packing. In an hour his plane would leave for Estes Park, Colorado. As Jerry took suitcases to the car I slipped my letter into his attaché case. *He'll discover it after he's on the plane,* I thought; *something to contemplate while he's away.*

My beloved Jerry,

You are wonderful! I am coming to love you as I loved you in the first springs and summers of our romance—fervently and deeply. You can't possibly know what that means to me. But for one thing it means (from a purely selfish point of view) that I may, after all, someday have someone who can really know me, really understand me—a best friend. I have tried to convince myself that probably the Lord wanted me to have that intimacy only with Him—that it is self-centered to want it or expect it of another human being. And maybe it is, I haven't quite found any justification, specifically anyway, for that in Scripture yet.

Just dreaming one night when you were away I put down on paper a description of the kind of relationship I would like to have with you if it were possible to have my most extravagant desires. Ignoring reality and our own limitations I included everything I'd ever want or enjoy in a marriage/friendship. Then I just sat and cried.

Then I asked myself a lot of questions:

—Why did I crave a relationship like this?

—Had the Lord planted the desire in me to motivate me to pursue a relationship like that with *Him*?

—Does this have anything to do with what He originally planned marriage to accomplish?

—Am I just thinking selfishly, focusing on *my* wants for things like companionship and understanding? (I've always taught that the wife's role was to *give* and to serve and not to put expectations or demands on her husband.)

—Did I have any basis for just ignoring your desires, whatever they might be, and blatantly asking God to *give me* such a relationship with you?

So, I've just left it for a while while I look to see if there are answers to these questions in the Word.

At any rate, I now feel that we have a possibility for at least a fairly close relationship—and that's a big jump from the lonely position I have been in. In the last few days it has come clearer to me what's taken place.

We married with a pretty well-balanced relationship—neither of us was overly dominant and we were able to talk and share each other's desires and goals. I never felt we were competing or fighting for control. We each *believed* in the other's dreams; since you weren't intimidated by me (or nagged), it didn't bother you to encourage me to do things independently of you (like radio, or speaking, etc.). We each had freedom and respect.

But when I began to read more and more about what men were like and how I should relate to make you happy, a gradual switch came in my attitudes. I honestly felt that to be loved I had to relate to you as a father figure whose duty before God was to correct me, lead, protect, provide for me and that I was one of the more fortunate women in that you were so good to me—allowing me to do many things other women can't do. Also, you give me enough money to meet my needs. Well, you know I've tried my best; it meant just learning to deny myself more and submit more. Seeing the whole picture now, it's obvious why a communication problem developed and why we lost the closeness and sharing.

When I realized that we had lost that closeness I didn't know why, and certainly took wrong approaches to solving it—demanding you talk to me, asking irritating questions. Those methods only increased the gap. And a very deep sorrow (that's the only way I know to say approximately what I began to feel) took over my attitude. It felt like, "the glory has departed!"; not only does my husband not love me, the real me—he has no idea of what I'm like. I have lost the capacity to emotionally love him. We never questioned the commitment aspect, of course. Now I can see that the intimacy I once enjoyed was somehow connected with my feelings of being understood, enjoyed, able to share what I thought and felt. It wasn't just the infatuation of young love.

Of course I wondered if this was just what happened to marriage after several years—two people simply found it too hard to share themselves so they found ways of living together without intimacy (at anything other than a sexual level). No wonder I saw dried up, dead marriages in people older than we—they were just toughing it on agape! Which is what I would have to do too!

I don't know where you're at in these areas or what you really want from me. I know it's impossible to say to you, "Please know me, please try to understand me." Those things can't happen by demanding or even, I think, by begging God to change another person's will. It's a selfish demand but I'm just telling you where I think I'm at in case you want some of the same things. What I'm happy about is that I'm starting to feel a release from that feeling of sorrow and I am beginning to *feel* strongly toward you—not just admiration, or awe, or concern, but genuine emotional love.

Sorry for rambling on so long. Guess you don't really need a whole book to hear me say

I love you,
Barbara

Reading that on the plane Jerry reflected on the emotions *he* was feeling. It seemed that deep changes were going on inside, upheaval foreign to the man he knew as himself. The concepts he discovered that week became another point of growth; another stage in the renewing of our minds that God counted essential in our steps to find each other again.

The following Saturday Jerry came home a very different husband. He brought the following two pieces of writing about himself as an attempt to explain:

Sharing

I have wondered at sharing—between two persons.
I have longed
and tried

and failed;
wondered,
tried,
failed . . .
A discovery!
(only mine—the facts of sharing are well known by everyone but me).
I asked
why, after conversation
even good and interesting,
for me there is so little fulfillment?
(I have fled from the boredom of mere
conversation.)
I leave perfectly artistic conversations
empty and . . .
disgusted.
(Sometimes I even leave [mentally] before they are finished—having already felt the usual tinge of boredom.)
"You are selfish, egotistical and a bore," I have declared to myself
(all of which may be the case).
The declaration, however, is far from the cure . . . and, I hope, some distance from the truth.

I looked from a distance
I saw my love—
graceful,
confident,
beautiful,
the object of envious eyes
talking—laughing—enjoying—
I longed to be in her world—the world of . . .
(I don't know the name of it; how, then shall I journey there?)

I will speak to her—
I will share my life—
I rehearsed the *facts* of my experience.
She, with patience, listened—responded
and all was quiet and empty.
It was late.
Dark.
I was far away—I needed
to hear her voice!
A few numbers on the dial and her voice . . .
We exchanged facts.
We seemed to reach across the lines to find
each other.
But just before the embrace we
always had to go.
No demand of time or money;
we had come to the
end, but had not arrived.

Suddenly the answer,
The discovery;
can something so simple be so great a revelation?
I do not need facts!
What my love *did* today is important
and interesting.
What I longed for was—
What did my love *feel* today?
What were her emotions?
Were you tired? Why?
Were you laughing? At what?
Did you feel a slight loss in my
absence? And
what is it you missed?

The facts of my love's life were only a
simple report.
A log.
A journal entry.
That which transforms the report into
sharing are the emotions,
the feelings
(those glimpses, however slight,
into the soul)
that accompanied those
events in the report.
But . . .
Sharing is two people exposing their feelings.
(Reporting is so much safer—there is no
risk in reporting.
The facts stand.)

My dear—
I have taken the safer route.
I have lapsed into reporting
and in so doing have lost touch with
my own emotions . . .
I have forced you to report . . . it seems to me
there is not the possibility of understanding each
other on the basis of the facts—

My earliest recollections of you, dearest, are not
facts.
I remember the ferryboats and the blue
coat and the
warm summer afternoons and the
canoes
flowers
and hikes in the
woods—
these things have meaning only in that

they call forth my *feeling* for you.
Suddenly my heart was feeling—
The ferryboat—I had ridden perhaps hundreds—that was only significant in that I was experiencing the first awesome and frightening pangs of newborn love!
Summer afternoons have happened forever.
I don't remember them all.
But the inexpressible (and irrepressible)
feelings of desire to embrace and become immersed in the life of the beautiful girl with whom I shared
that summer afternoon
make the event cast in permanence
To log our locations would be an impoverished
history of our love.

But somewhere—I can't find the exact spot (maybe unimportant)—
I reduced my life to reporting—
I reported to people—
People reported to me—
People reported about me.
No time to feel.
Even if time permitted there was
no time to analyze the feeling
and put it in communicable form.
Little hints were left as to what feelings
were being experienced,
but they were increasingly few and
vague;
predictably they were misinterpreted

and finally stopped altogether.
Thus the "creeping separateness."
I not only lost you—I lost myself.
I began to actually believe the nonsense
that men don't feel—they think.
Life became cerebral and devastatingly
empty.
The middle years of our love, unlike the
beginnings,
are filled with places, things, facts
but no feelings—
a travelog but no pulse—
Australia, Hawaii, London—
exotic, romantic.
Early on in our love I would have covered
Australian sand with romantic, even
erotic love
and remembered not just beaches
but embraces and laughter and
daydreaming and chasing.
But I didn't know how you *felt*.
I didn't know how to get in touch with my
feelings.
So I reduced the experience to
reporting—
slides—
facts.

(I am embarrassed at this intolerable rambling.
If you are still reading
you have proven your love
beyond *all* doubt.)
What is happening, my dear, is precisely this:
Through a series of emotionally traumatic
experiences—God is quickening again my emotions.

The incredible pressure of the church all this
year has driven me into utter helplessness
before Him.
The total depression and incredulity of what seemed to me an unsalvageable marriage and the
accompanying sense of complete failure
(These are all *emotions*; I was *feeling* these events; it
was not reporting, thus shocking my dead
passions into life again).
The frustrated helplessness of feeling utterly misunderstood
yet seeing that I had salted the very confusion.
The anguish of seeing the love and focus
of my life unable to survive in my presence.
The confusion and guilt of speaking as though
having answers yet living with a growing
emptiness.
The disappointment of my failure as a father
coming simultaneously with the
irrepressible joy of Sundar's arrival.
The Hong Kong Experience—the
Severe Mercy coming at the end of all this
and no way found to communicate.

And now, Estes Park!

I came to it through the emotional load of an entire year
when a resurrection of emotional life was being called
from the tomb of my being.
It was 1:00 A.M., there were no lights,
no one awake.
I burst like a fountain—sobs—

I ran from our room, so as not to
wake my roommate
(actually, so as not to have
to explain).
For the next hour the dead emotions of my life were
spoken into life. I wept, feeling very manly.
What is all of this?

My dear,
I want you to know not just the facts of my life, I
want you to know my feelings. I have not
known there was a distinction before (how
ignorant I feel). I have had no feelings, I
have only classified information.
Christ in His love is shocking my feelings back to
life.
Estes Park thus far is a mass of feelings. Of
tears on my cheeks
at the name of Jesus,
of emotional longings for
you,
of emotional love for
others.

My fear as I close this is that
somehow it is beyond me.
Perhaps I have damaged you so desperately
with my reporting that you cannot
risk
your feelings to me.
Perhaps I will not take the ultimate
risk and tell you this: This is a beginning.
Please walk with me.

I have spoken of sharing,
My dearest,
Don't be put off by my ineptness—let us somehow learn to share. I'll start:
Here are my feelings just now
about you:
I deeply love you and am
feeling love.
Could it be we are
falling in love?

Rebirth of Beautiful Blue

It's familiar . . .
somewhere in the distant past a
ferryboat whistles—
sea air washes clean
and I see her
still in blue—
Beautiful Blue.
She seems more graceful now,
a slight touch of elegance
not a girl, or a lady
the glowing reality of womanhood.
No light thing . . .
these feelings I have;
once they were "first true love"
now—
deep—
knowing—
mellow.
It is true!!
It is love reborn
though more like
metamorphosis. (unromantic term!)

The cocoon of experience—
the tearing apart—
the bringing back together—
Emerging new life, all that the old
was but worlds more.

I remember
in the breeze
salt air
blowing tresses—
"I love you."
Now
How can identical words carry such
new meaning
(A tiny man from China,
bent,
hurting, speaking.
"I love Jesus," he said;
I spoke those words, but he from depths beyond my world).

On the bow I spoke long ago—
"I love you."
So now, my dearest, from depths beyond that world
I love you

Questions for Discussion

After reading this chapter can you identify some possible reasons for loneliness among women in what would traditionally be called good marriages?

Jerry referred to a common belief that "men don't feel, they think." How do you view that belief in our culture? If it is true of men, *should* it be? How does Jesus' personality compare to this definition of masculinity?

Why is it safer to report than to share feelings?

ENDINGS?/Jerry

Where do we end a book on relationships? If we were dealing with mere reporting of data or changeless formulas, I suppose the end would be obvious. But we are dealing with persons—persons in the process of growth and change. Even while this book has been in process, new discoveries have flooded our lives, changing and maturing our own marriage.

What are the bottom-line items that do not change? We have spoken some about form but, as we have seen, form does and should change. It seems to me that the constant that must stand is not the form or the discussions of role or any set of rules or standards. What must be utterly secure is the commitment that two persons have made to each other. This commitment is not the mere invention of the emotional moment, for even that emotion will change. It is the commitment of two persons to love each other according to the 1 Corinthians 13 definition. A love that is not only voiced but translated into life-style by the constant choice of the lover and the beloved. A commitment that says and lives—

I will be patient with you;
I will be kind to you;
I will not envy you;
I will not boast or proudly
elevate myself above you;
I will not be rude to you;
I will not exploit you for my
own selfish ends;
I will not be easily angered
with you;
I will keep no record of wrongs;
I will not delight when you are harmed,
or I hear evil concerning you;
I will rejoice with truth;
I will always protect you;
I will always trust you;
I will always hope in you;
I will persevere with you;
I will never fail you.

(see 1 Cor. 13:4-8a)

Such a commitment to you will be kept for life for I choose not to live without you ever again. My inability to keep such an ideal is covered by the marvelous beauty of forgiveness. I can blow it and be forgiven. That is not license, that is freedom to grow without intimidation.

Barbara and I do not feel we have a perfect marriage. That is not why we have written this book—to tell of our perfect marriage and how you too can have one like it! But because we are learning to forgive each other and ourselves for not having a perfect marriage, for not being a perfect wife and husband, we are excited about our future. We're not afraid of failure. Even our failures can be redeemed, turned into something valuable for God to work with. In fact, it's mainly our failures that we've shared with you on these pages. Our weaknesses and frustrations are the materials God uses to teach us His ideas about this relationship. Our frustrations were good—they were not the problem, they were the stimulus to open our eyes and see the shifting sands upon which we had tried to build a marriage. Thankfully, we also had some good rocks in our foundation. Love and commitment were there even though we weren't always sure what they meant. Some of our erroneous ideas about romance, femininity, paternalism and ideal marriage standards were very unsteady foundations. We have freely showed you some of our emotions and doubts about other "sandy" areas. If you've read this as a married person, hopefully you've been alerted to parts of your own foundations that are sandy. And they've not necessarily been identical to ours.

What God wants is not to tear the house down and start from scratch. He wants to replace misconceptions with truth, fantasy with reality, wrong assumptions with authentic communication. As two people grow into becoming who they really are in Christ, they find their marriage a becoming thing—an experience of relationship in process. Deep fellowship becomes a strong block in the foundation, experienced in sharing goals, conversations, sexual pleasure, and spiritual life.

We do not yet know what our new house will look like. The foundation is becoming more solid every day. We think most of the sand has been dug out and replaced, but God may yet have work unknown to us left to do in strengthening the base. One thing we know so far—our new home is roomier.

Barbara hated the idea of moving to another house when Jamie was born. She liked the one we lived in. But it was terribly cramped. Our family had simply outgrown it, we needed more room. Now, of course, she loves the big house and all the wide open spaces. She drives past the old one and wonders why she ever wanted to stay there!

We feel the same way about our marriage. The new foundation can support a much larger house, needed by two growing people. It can also support a house that will withstand stress. Wind, water, earthquakes, adversity can only strengthen this relationship.

This simple illustration pictures what I've been saying about foundations. It doesn't include all the things we've discussed as faulty foundations or as biblical foundations. It's merely a visualization of concepts we've presented. You can think about your own marriage and picture the blocks that need to be added to what we've placed here. We've discussed the place of emotions and their expression, closeness, intimacy, security and other elements of relationship.

"Therefore everyone who hears these words of mine and puts them into practice is like a wise man who built his house on the rock. The rain came down, the streams rose, and the winds blew and beat against that house; yet it did not fall, because it had its foundation on the rock. But everyone who hears these words of mine and does not put them into practice is like a foolish man who built his house on sand. The rain came down, the streams rose, and the winds blew and beat against that house, and it fell with a great crash" (Matt. 7:24-27).

A MARRIAGE BUILT ON SAND

Fulfillment Money Paternalism Career

Romance Maternalism Sexual Attraction

Role Expectations	Cultural Values	Performance
Peer Expectations	i.e. "Ideal Marriage"	Possessiveness
Conditional "Love"		Emotions

A MARRIAGE BUILT ON THE ROCK
(CHRIST'S TEACHINGS)

Love	Acceptance	Forgiveness
Living for God & His Purposes	Authentic Knowing (Real People)	Christ's Authority & Lordship
Value of Each Person	Sharing Life	Deep Fellowship
Trust	Commitment	Mutual Submission

I really am not overly concerned about the form of your marriage. You may choose the vertical relationship where the husband's authority is supreme. You may have a more modified view or an equal partnership. My concern is that whatever the form, you both are totally fulfilling the commitment which marriage involves. All else must stand in line behind that value. We must declare with our lives, "I love you," and let all else stand aside while that commitment is fulfilled.

While considering all of this one day I felt the frustration of time. As Barbara and I were reaching out for each other again and sensing the undiluted joy of living together as friends and lovers, I became increasingly aware of the pressure of time and my inclination to view it as an enemy!

I expressed something of my frustration and the beginnings of a solution in the following lines:

The Nature of Love and Time

A rare delicacy touches her soft cheek;
she's no common girl.
There is a gentle elegance in her step,
that charming elegance that loses no warmth.

I often quietly observe her:
Charm is not alone in clothes
or sophistication;
it seems to crown the simple things . . .
a look
a touch
a smile
the conveyance of beauty through being.

The tragedy of our love is time . . .
it takes time to capture the reality of
delicacy and elegant charm.

Yet . . .
we may struggle with time or
embrace Him.
He may be our guard at the prison gate
or our liberator into each other.

As the hours seldom come to quietly observe
you—my love

I shall liberate the moments and drink
of your touch
your smile
your look . . .

And consider great wealth those hours—
even (God grant) days
when, alone at last,
we shall be enfolded by the warmth
and beauty of our love.

I seriously doubt that the experiences Barbara and I have had are normative or that our discussions really are in any way conclusive. Our tendencies to write love letters and prose to each other, or to express ourselves in romantic picture language, are not necessarily elements you need in your marriage. You may have established better ways of communicating—better for you, that is. Each relationship is unique; each pairing of two persons is unique. Our habits of study and philosophizing together are just part of us, something we've risked sharing with you.

This book is our way of saying, PLEASE DON'T STOP THE DIALOGUE ON MARRIAGE. Let's keep asking and learning and seeking. Unless someone keeps the subject open, we too easily draw shallow conclusions that rob us of all God intended. We won't be unhappy if you read this and feel no inclination to agree with us; but we hope you do feel an inclination to think and grow.

If you have walked through these pages with us and found yourself having to evaluate, examine and elevate your sights on your marriage, then we have, in some measure, succeeded.

Paul, in writing to the Roman church, has also written a fitting benediction for our marriages: "May the God who gives endurance and encouragement give you a spirit of unity among yourselves as you follow Christ Jesus, so that with one heart and mouth you may glorify the God and Father of our Lord Jesus Christ. Accept one another, then, just as Christ accepted you, in order to bring praise to God" (Rom. 15:5-7).